Calling All Lightpreneurs™

Your help is needed

Calling All Lightpreneurs™
Your help is needed

By Elmas Vincent

lightpreneur™ Publishing

Lightpreneurs™ Publishing
16211 N Scottsdale Road #246
Scottsdale, AZ 85254
www.lightpreneurpublishing.com

Ordering Information:
Special discounts are available on quantity purchases by corporations, associations, and others. For details, contact the publisher at the address above.
Printed in the United States of America

This book is designed to provide information and motivation to our readers. It is sold with the understanding that the author or publisher is not engaged to render any type of psychological, legal, or any other kind of professional advice. No warranties or guarantees are expressed or implied by the publisher's choice to include any of the content in this volume. Neither the publisher nor the author shall be liable for any physical, psychological, emotional, financial, or commercial damages, including, but not limited to, special, incidental, consequential or other damages. Our views and rights are the same: You are responsible for your own choices, actions, and results. Every business is different and the information and strategies contained herein may not be suitable for your situation. You should seek the services of a competent professional before beginning any program.

Vincent, Elmas.
Calling All Lightpreneurs™ :

ISBN 978-0-615-48969-8
1. Spirituality 2. Buiness
First Edition

For my mother, Mae "The Angel Lady"

Thank you for showing me what
unconditional love truly is

Acknowledgments:

Thank you to the following people who helped bring this book to life and to smooth out the crazy professors craziness:

Michelle Knight, Holly Peterson and Arlene Puro

Thank you to all of my clients for teaching me what a Lightpreneur™ is, the best ways to help you and just how special you all are.

Thank you Janine for bearing with me during *my* Lightpreneur™ journey - even through the bumpy parts.

A special thank you to Cindy Thelen for joining me on this journey of creating the Calling All Lightpreneurs™ book. Here it is.

Table of Contents

Forward

KC Miller

"What do you want to be when you grow up?" is a question asked of children, teens, and even adults.

One of my most vivid memories is being asked this question in the third grade. Without hesitation I said, "I want to own my own business." The teacher paused for just a moment, then smiled and said, "So, you want to be an entrepreneur, do you?" Never having heard the word entrepreneur before, I did not fully capture the word in my mind. For quite some time thereafter, when asked the age-old question, "What do you want to be when you grow up?" I would say, "I want to be a 'preneur.'"

I did grow up to own several businesses, one of which is an award-winning private college dedicated to helping people discover their gifts and supporting their efforts to start their own business or private practices. One of my greatest joys and delights is to see graduates create a business from the training and skills they receive at Southwest Institute of Healing Arts. Some take the information they receive and just soar with it, while others seem to be grounded in the fear of having to market themselves. They cannot even begin to imagine themselves as a "salesperson"; to them it's as if sales and marketing are dirty words, and some look at them as less than appealing activities.

The students who attend Southwest Institute of Healing Arts tend to dive very deep into their passions and have a strong desire to serve. Students train in a variety of healing modalities, from massage and energy work, to life coaching and hypnotherapy. Often this takes them on a very personal and sometimes spiritual path. As their

11

talents are emerging and their passion for their practice deepens, the more "in service" they choose to become. For some, the thought of actually charging clients seems out of line with their "mission" to touch and heal lives.

In the search for highly qualified and motivated instructors to help teach the Entrepreneurial Support classes offered at the college, I had the good fortune to meet Elmas Vincent during a Life Coaching training session. His passion and commitment to train budding business owners matched mine, plus it was coupled with his impressive formal academic credentials of having an MBA.

It was a goose-bump/God-bump kind-of-a-day when Elmas handed me a postcard that featured his newest revelation: *Lightpreneurs*! Tears filled my eyes, my flesh swelled with confirmation, and my heart was full with excitement. YES, that is exactly the type of "preneur" I had always dreamed of being--a "Lightpreneur™."

Without needing to hear another word, I realized that Elmas had captured the functional essence of working with gifted healers and highly trained practitioners who saw themselves one way, yet needed to be another way in the world of marketing and promotion.

In this book *Lightpreneurs*™, Elmas has an amazing way of connecting with you and helping you understand that honoring your passion and your work CAN be done through sales and marketing. The ease with which he shows you how to reach more people, be more successful, and live your dream of touching and healing even MORE lives is enlightening, to say the least. He teaches you how to be a "Lightpreneur™"!

My message is always: pray to God and row the boat. This book is a manual for rowing the boat.

What I love most is that Elmas Vincent fully acknowledges the creative forces that are working on all dimensions. He honors the spiritual nature of the various healing practices and yet knows in the depth of his heart that there are practical steps that must be taken to bring dreams into reality. It's a little like wanting to eat the most delicious angel food cake: If you buy all the ingredients, yet never assemble them and put them into the oven to bake, you will never be able to create a mouth-watering angel food cake.

Lightpreneur™ is definitely a way to have your cake and eat it too! You have the ingredients, Elmas gives you the recipe, and now it's time to put it all together...and enjoy your sweet success.

Introduction

The Journey...

This book is the result of a journey. My journey. So who am I and why should you care?

My name is Elmas Vincent. Growing up, my family owned a chain of clothing stores. Many mornings as a child I awoke in a merchandise counter in one of our stores and would go directly from there to school because my mother and father had worked through the night. My father had a massive coronary by the time he was 40 years old. The last thing I ever wanted to do at that point was be a business owner. At the time, owning a business to me meant working 80, 90, or 100-plus hours per week with enormous stress.

Off to college I went, with my father dreaming of me coming back to run the family business. My dreams were quite different. I became a professional student taking every class imaginable. In my second senior year of college, it appeared that my dream of being a professional marathon runner might not come true. The corporate world seemed like the best alternative. With a degree blending industrial engineering and management,

I did not feel quite ready to jump on the corporate ladder, so I chose to study for my MBA at Tulane University. The MBA program at Tulane was the perfect fit. It was specifically geared to the corporate world, and it had a great track record of its graduates doing well in that arena.

It is my belief that _____ (fill in your word for the higher power) has an amazing sense of humor. Why else would I end up as the teaching and research assistant for the professor trying to create one of the first university-level courses on owning a business? Why else would I end up helping create a course on entrepreneurship? Why else would I end up teaching part of that class? At the time, it seemed like such a distraction and even an injustice. This had nothing to do with grooming me for the corporate world.

After Tulane and suffering through the indignity of working on a class about entrepreneurship, it was off to the corporate world. After only a few years, I was wondering why corporate America was ever appealing at all. The politics, the games, all started to feel very much out of character with who I really was. It started to dawn on me, thinking back to the information from researching and creating that class at Tulane: you do not have to work yourself to death to own a business. It was all about leverage and systems and doing business the smart way. So I left the corporate world and never looked back. Since then, I have started numerous businesses. along the way discovering that I love the aspect of starting a business—the challenge, the creativity, the rush. But, I don't really like running businesses. It always became boring and tedious after it was actually up and running. That was before Lightpreneurs™.

As a child I was very "spiritual." At a very early age, my beliefs of the world, how things worked—behind the scenes, so to speak—and God had already formed. I was a voracious reader who read things that were not the norm for that age, culture, and environment. By my teen years, it became apparent that my beliefs and spirituality did not serve me based on the culture around me. So, all that was put on a shelf for many years.

After a very trying time in my life, I took that spirituality off the shelf, dusted it off, and again fully embraced it. It was during that period of stepping back into spirituality that I learned my name actually had a meaning. Having only met one other "Elmas" before, my father, it always was assumed that Elmas was just a unique name. Then, in my 30s with a "chance" encounter, it was revealed that my name has a meaning. It is actually the Turkish word for "diamond." By the way, I fully believe that there are NO coincidences. It was no coincidence that when I had just passed through the darkest period of my life and embraced my truth again that I learned that every time someone calls me by my name, they are calling me a "diamond."

My journey has taken me full circle. Seemingly unrelated, disjointed aspects of my life have come together like a complex puzzle that was difficult to see at first, just looking at all the individual pieces. I now have a business that combines all the aspects of my journey: the valleys and peaks, my education and experiences, things I could never have imagined being related. This is a business that could never be boring because I get to help create hundreds of businesses each year. I get to use all of those puzzle pieces as a wonderful, finished portrait to help other people realize that no matter what they think of themselves, they are a diamond inside and can spread their light to create impact for the world.

Now this book uses all of the pieces from my journey, my education, and the seemingly random "lessons" of life to help other Lightpreneurs™ on their journey. So what is this book actually about?

This book is about being a Lightpreneur™.

A Lightpreneur™ is an Entrepreneur of Light, shining to illuminate the truth for others, a lighthouse providing safe passage in what may appear to be treacherous waters. A Lightpreneur™ is a role model, showing that business can be done from a place of light, love, and integrity. A Lightpreneur™ exemplifies the principles of abundance in the universe by receiving just as freely as giving.

This book is about realizing there is no contradiction.

Giving and receiving are both equal parts of the same thing, the yin and yang, the balance. The "business" is just the way the Lightpreneur™ receives and so is able to give even more light, thus receiving even more in an ever-expanding cycle. The reality is there is no contradiction in being of light and being in business. It is just the structure of that exchange of giving and receiving. By giving and not receiving, an imbalance is created, harmony is diminished, and disease appears. In *Calling All Lightpreneurs™*, you will find ways to create harmony in your business.

This book is about overcoming FEAR.

Fear can paralyze. Fear can sabotage. We will spend a chapter together exposing fear for what it is—an illusion. No matter what your fears may be, no matter how big or small, it is better to identify them and call them out into the open. Fear is darkness and cannot stand before the light. We will shine light on fear.

This book is about SIMPLE tools to help your light business shine.

This is not a business textbook. There are plenty of those around. In our journey, you will discover simple concepts to help your business. Simple can be the most profound. We have clients who constantly cycle through the tools and concepts presented here, taking them deeper and wider into their businesses with each pass.

This book is about making the journey fun and easier.

What was your reaction to that statement? Did it make you smile? Did you mentally cross your arms in resistance? Did it give you hope? Why not fun? Why not easy? Does it make it more valuable if it is hard? I think not. Actually, quite the contrary. If it is hard, it shows the world that light is struggle. Just reading that sounds contradictory.

Sherpas

This is not the start of the journey. Your journey started a long time ago. This book just offers tools and instructions to make the journey you are already on easier and help move it toward more success. Just as the Sherpas do not climb Mount Everest for anyone, neither I nor this book could or should travel your journey for you. The climber chooses whether to listen to the Sherpa's advice. You choose what to take from this book, if anything. I have been on a journey myself and have been Sherpa to many Lightpreneurs™ before, and hopefully to many

19

more after. This book is my way of expanding Light more than possible one on one.

Open your mind to the concepts here. If they do not seem to apply at first, look at them from different angles to see what you can take from them and apply. Open your heart to the truth. You can do this. You have the ability, the courage, and the support if you are just open to it. Open your spirit and allow yourself to be all that you can be—all that you were meant to be. I look forward to hearing about your journey: the victories, the challenges, the joy.

Thank you for allowing me to be a part of your journey,

Elmas

Chapter 1

In The beginning...

How Lightpreneurs™ came to be

Most Lightpreneurs™ have an immediate reaction the first time they hear the term "Lightpreneur™." Even if they do not know what it really means, they **know** that it applies to them. The actual definition of "Lightpreneur™" is less meaningful than the energy that surrounds it. I will start out by talking about how the term actually came about.

I have been teaching and coaching entrepreneurs for several years, and I kept being led to work with practitioners and the spiritual, or what I now call the Lightpreneur™ Community. Even though I knew this was my purpose, my logical mind was extremely resistant to it. My logical mind wanted me to pick a niche which would be a lot easier to work with, one that, in general, was already more business-savvy and willing to do what it would take to be successful. But the universe had a different idea. It was determined to have me work with the Lightpreneur™ community. My purpose was to work with people who were not so business-oriented, but more people and spiritually oriented, to help them integrate that business aspect.

Here is how the term came about. In the spring of 2008, I was teaching a class to a group of prospective Lightpreneurs™, including coaches, energy workers, and other practitioners. There were about 20 participants, all women, in this daylong class. Whenever I would use terms like "entrepreneur," "marketing," or "business," they would immediately have an energetic reaction, and it was not necessarily a good one. I could tell that this group, as with many I had worked with before, had a complete resistance to anything "business." My logical mind was struggling with this because I knew that in order for them to be successful and continue doing what they loved and what they were supposed to do, they were going to have to look at the business aspects of their practice. As their resistance grew, so did my frustration. I did not know how to bridge that gap for this group.

My fears were further reinforced when we took a break and one of the participants came up to me and expressed her frustration and reluctance to anything "business." She went on to say that just the mere thought of being an entrepreneur paralyzed her. I was hesitant about even going back in the room. What was I going to say to these women? How was I going to help them overcome this hurdle in order to be successful? I went into the restroom and reset my intention for the highest and best for ALL involved and to be able to relay to these students whatever information they needed in order to take the next big step. When I went back into the room, I was looking across all of their faces, which expressed a mixture of fear, excitement, frustration, and anticipation. Each and every person in there wanted to move forward, but they were paralyzed by fear and resistance.

What came out of my mouth next was not planned in any way, and I certainly do not take credit for it because it did not come from me, but rather, *through* me. I said to them, "Do not think of yourselves as entrepreneurs. You are Lightpreneur™." The moment I said it, every face in the room shifted and I did not know at first if it was a good thing or a bad thing, but there was a look of shock on each and every face in the room. I was frozen and could not say anything else, and finally one of them spoke up and said, "That is it! That is exactly what I am!" I was trying to figure out exactly what "that" was, but then I heard myself elaborate and express to them that they are not just entrepreneurs. They are not creating a business for business' sake. They are not creating to profit, per se, but in order to create the abundance and prosperity they needed to keep doing what they loved doing and what they were sent here to do. They would have to be open to combining their gift with some basic business techniques so they could soar. For the rest of the day, the energy completely shifted. They were excited. They almost wanted to leave in that moment and go out and start creating their new Lightpreneur™ business. It gave them energy and released their paralysis so they could take immediate action.

After the day was over, the power of "Lightpreneurs™" scared me so much that I put it on a shelf and tried not to think about it. The universe had other ideas of course. I always say that the universe gives me three chances to act on what I am directed to do. The first one is a whisper in the ear. The second one is a tap on the shoulder. The third one is a two-by-four upside the head. I had already received the whisper long before. This was the tap on the shoulder, really pointing out that this was what I was supposed to be doing and these were the people I was supposed to be working with. But I didn't listen. Instead I waited for the two-by-four upside the head, and it came that fall.

Just before the holidays, I became ill and, being who I am, I ignored it. It started out as a persistent cough. Then I had a continuous fever that wouldn't seem to go away. Teaching became a struggle. I was normally able to teach all weekend and feel energized, but instead a four-hour class now was a struggle for me. Just being able to speak through the coughing and the congestion was a problem. I continued to get worse, and I continued to ignore it. As someone who normally only sleeps four to five hours a night, I suddenly found myself sleeping 12-14 hours a day, still exhausted when I awoke. Simple tasks that I had loved doing before became monumental undertakings that took all of my energy, and I'd have to go back and lay down just to recuperate. I had been whacked upside the head pretty good. And yet I continued to refuse to listen.

Finally my partner expressed to me that something had to change. This was not who I was, and both my life and my business were suffering too much for me to continue like that. When I finally discovered that a rather simple disease had overtaken my whole body, making my blood so acidic that even a small infection would ravage my body, I knew that something was up. Instead of looking to the traditional medical model, I turned inside myself and said, "What is this? Why am I experiencing this?" The answer became very clear. I was ignoring my purpose. I was ignoring the very reason I was here. The illness had forced me to stop. It kept me from all the busyness and made me listen to the truth.

I remembered the "Lightpreneur™" term. It had been dancing in the back of my mind for quite some time now. I did something not even knowing why I was doing it, but I made a little mention of it on Facebook. The response was overwhelming. Just the mere mention of the term "Lightpreneur™" excited people. They wanted to know what it was and if that was what they were, even though they already knew the answer. It created a buzz that I could not have predicted in any way. I tried to hide again, but it just didn't happen. The genie was out of the bottle, and now the universe was bringing people to me, demanding that Lightpreneurs™ come to life. Everywhere I went and mentioned the word "Lightpreneur™," people had to know more. They wanted to know how it applied to them. They were excited about the prospect of being a Lightpreneur™.

So what is a Lightpreneur™? Here is the raw definition:

-noun—a person who organizes an enterprise focused on creating a positive impact in the world. Light refers to the spiritual aspect of letting your light shine as brightly as possible and, in so doing, illuminating the world to be a brighter, better place, and -preneur refers to creating a business around that so you can keep shining that light and do it in even bigger ways.

–verb--to act as a lightpreneur™.

So the definition is quite dry, but the energy of aLightpreneur™ as someone who is doing their business, living their purpose, and leaving the world a little better than when they first got here, is electric. A Lightpreneur™ could actually be any type of business, but for the purpose of this book and the coaching that I do, I focus mostly on people who are in what I refer to as the healing arts. That is a broad, encompassing term, but it refers to everything from naturopathic doctors, to energy workers, to speakers to life coaches, and many others. A Lightpreneur™ does not have to ask if they are a Lightpreneur™. They already know it. As soon as they hear the term, it resonates with them. What is a Lightpreneur™? Chances are if you are reading this book, it is you. If not in this moment, then it is what you are supposed to be in the very near future. So, Lightpreneur™, come join me on this journey.

Chapter 2

Calling All Lightpreneurs™
Why we need you now more than ever

I want to pose a question to you. Why do we need Lightpreneurs now more than ever? I am sure you can come up with many reasons. The world is in a huge state of flux. If you look at any aspect of our modern world, I do not think anyone would contest that there's change going on and more change is on the way. Whether you look at the economy, the environment, politics, stability of various countries, religion, the nuclear family, values in general, morals, ethics, or the business world, there's a lot of uncertainty in the world, and with uncertainty comes fear.

I like the acronym for fear: False Evidence Appearing Real. In the moment, for most people, fear seems very real. People fear change. Right now there is change all around us. Every aspect of our lives has some kind of change going on. There's instability everywhere. Whether you are looking at the micro or the macro environment, there's massive change going on all around us. In my opinion, we as a society have many choices to make—choices involving all the areas I just spoke of, including environment, politics, business, and basically how we live our lives. I feel that through the ages, all these things are like a pendulum that swings from one side back to the other, and I do not think either left or right is necessarily right or wrong. However, the optimum place for us to be is somewhere in the middle.

We are in danger in a lot of areas right now, of either falling back to the way things were, or going so far in the other direction that it's going to be detrimental to our society. We cannot just throw away all of the gains we've made, technologically, socially, and in every other way, just because it's been difficult recently. We have to embrace those changes and figure out what's best for everyone. This is where Lightpreneurs™ of all types come into play.

Instead of looking at the world in judgment and in terms of what's wrong, Lightpreneurs™ can lead the way to what's right. Lightpreneurs™ can help others to embrace love rather than fear and to love rather than hate. That is truly what a Lightpreneur™ is all about, in my opinion, to move business, society, the environment, and everything to a place of love. If we operate from that place of love, it will be very difficult to make bad decisions. In fear, it's very easy to make bad decisions. You consciously make good decisions by looking at intention and emotion. If your intentions feel like love, then that is where you are coming from. If you feel anything else—judgment, anger, disgust, etc.—then you are not serving the world as the true Lightpreneur™ that you know you are.

Think back to some of the people who remind you of what this looks like. It might be Gandhi, Mother Teresa, or Nelson Mandela. Even in the harshest of situations, they always approached their circumstances with love. Even when Nelson Mandela and Gandhi were in prison, they didn't act as prisoners. They acted with feelings of love and compassion toward those who imprisoned them. They persevered through everything with kindness, rather than being angry at their situation. Mother Teresa never set out to create the movement she created. She only wanted to make a space where the unloved felt loved. Everything about Mother Teresa boiled down to acts of love and compassion.

So when you are dealing with a difficult situation in your life or your practice, take a moment and breathe and check in and ask yourself—what is my emotion in this moment? What is my intention? If you are coming from a place of love and compassion, then you will say and do the right things. But if you are coming from any other emotion, it's moving you away from your true self, stripping you of your power, and affecting your practice, your business, and every aspect of what you do and what you represent in this world. Teaching your clients about how to live in the world this way plays a major part of the Lightpreneur's™ journey.

If you are a Lightpreneur™, it is time to step up. Now is the time. Our world is in flux. We are in a time of great change. Now is the time to help the world embrace love and make the positive choices. Now is the time for you to step as fully into your light, into your business, as you possibly can and magnify that light so that you can create a bigger impact on even more people. That is what being a Lightpreneur™ is all about. It's helping to magnify the impact and the light and create the biggest, positive change we possibly can. Are you ready to step up as a

Lightpreneur™? I hope so. If so, continue reading. That is what we want to do. To help you magnify your own light so you can magnify the light of the world.

Chapter 3

Abundant Gifts
A New Paradigm

I would imagine that most of the people reading this book feel they do have a gift to offer to the world. They have a gift that was essentially given to them. I want you to think for a moment about who that giver is. You can label it anything you want: God, Universe, Mother Nature. It does not matter what name you choose, who you call the Giver that gave you that gift. But They have an intention for that gift that They gave you.

Let me clarify what I mean by "a gift." Some people have a gift of being able to help other people by coaching them to live life to their potential. Others see or hear or know information that can help people on their path. Some are good with energy healing or clearing blocks. Maybe your gift is creating. Whatever it is, I imagine you feel you have some kind of gift that is part of your purpose in this world and that you are supposed to share with the world.

Universe, God, Creator, or whatever your source is that you feel gave you that gift, had an intention when you came into this world. Let's look at a scenario for a moment. Do you think this was the intention for your amazing ability to impact people's lives? For the Creator to say, "Here's what's going to happen. You are to go out and get a job to pay the rent and the bills and keep the lights on and put food on the table. You are supposed to work this job 40 hours and then commute another 10-15 hours per week. Then when you get home, even though you are tired, you have to take care of your family. So in any given week, you must put in 70-80 hours that have nothing to do with your gift. Now with any left over time you have, you are to use *that* time to share your gift and its benefit with the world."

Does that seem like reality to you? In my belief, that was not the intention of your Creator, your God, whoever gave you this gift. That wasn't the intention at all for you to be given this gift and have you waste the majority of your life working a job just for the sole purpose of paying the bills for the material things you are told that you need. I believe you were given those gifts with the expectation that you would also *receive* in the giving of that gift. They gave you the gift expecting you to go out and share it with the world and create prosperity for yourself first so you could become the example for what it means to live a purposeful life. You become the example of prosperity. You become the example of possibility. It wasn't given to you to squander it away while you do things that are totally unrelated to your calling.

What I am going to encourage you to do here is to honor whoever gave you that gift; honor God, honor Christ, honor your Creator, honor whoever it is by using your gift with pride and expecting to receive back as an exchange for sharing that gift. Expect to create prosperity in your own life first so you are the example. You are the possibility for whom you are working with. If you are to have an impact on people's lives, you need to live in the example of how it's done, not in poverty, but in prosperity. I encourage you, I implore you, to go out and use your gift with pride. I encourage you to go out and create abundance for yourself. I encourage you to go out and be the light that you were created to be. If you are a Lightpreneur™, you already know that you are here, in part, to guide others on their path to their gifts and light. But first you must step in and claim your own.

In most native cultures there is the "medicine man / woman" figure. This person is responsible for the well-being of the tribe: spiritually, physically, and mentally. In my opinion, they are the equivalent of most Lightpreneurs™ for modern society. By the way, I use the term "modern society" very loosely here. It does not necessarily indicate better. In most tribes the shaman or medicine man is highly respected and usually the wealthiest member of the tribe. Their every need is attended to without question or asking. Their huts are cleaned when they are away. Food is prepared for and served to them. Anything they require is automatically provided so they are not distracted from what they need to do. As the modern medicine men and women, I believe you deserve to have all of these needs met without stress or distraction also. Money is just the energy with which these things are fulfilled in our society. Accept it, embrace it.

Lightpreneur™, allow your light to shine as brightly as possible by allowing prosperity to flow through you. Be that example. Accept your gifts as freely as you give yours.

Chapter 4

Types of Entrepreneurs
Knowing Your Type Makes Your Journey Easier

In working with entrepreneurs for many years now, I normally classify them into three basic categories. Some entrepreneurs will actually cross over into more than one category, but I find that most people have a primary category that they fall into.

The first of these categories is called the **Weather Vane** entrepreneur. I am sure you have seen pictures of weather vanes. They are usually in the form of a chicken or rooster sitting up on top of an arrow with the N/S/E/W designation for the four directions. They are also known as copulas. They point in the direction that the wind is blowing.

The reason I call this category of entrepreneurs the "Weather Vane" entrepreneur is because these people have new ideas constantly. Their problem is not a lack of ideas; it is having **too many** ideas. They are constantly pointing in a new direction any time a new idea comes up. They have a new idea and they chase it for a period of time, but then another idea comes along and they think that is the best thing. So they start chasing that one for a little while, then it is off to another and another and another.

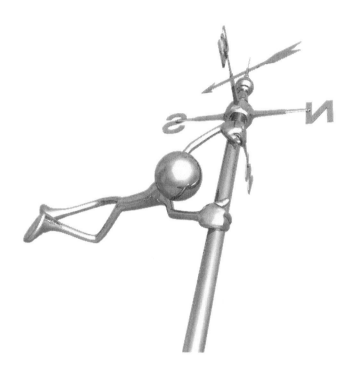

I am sure that many people reading this book right now are laughing to themselves because this is so familiar to them. They know that this is a challenge to them as they have not been able to focus long enough to create success in their business. That is their main challenge, their lack of focus. In order to succeed in business, you are going to have to focus. You are going to have to see it through to success. Instead of going after a new idea every time a challenge comes up, you will need to work through the challenge because any new idea is going to have challenges also.

I love my Weather Vanes dearly because I can easily fall into the trap of being a Weather Vane entrepreneur. I have those same challenges, and I, too, can constantly chase new ideas. Anyone who knows me knows that I can have 12 different things going on at once.

The real key for the Weather Vane entrepreneur is taking an idea or picking a category of ideas and committing to seeing them through to success--to their completion. But then the question comes up: how do you stop the idea flow? Understand that I do not want you to stop it. I want you to continue that flow. I want you to continue having as many amazing ideas as you can. But instead of chasing each and every one, I want you to write them down. I do not care if it is on a napkin or a slip of paper— just make a record of them. Then create a folder to put those ideas in and allow them to accumulate over time. I like to do business in 90-day cycles. So every 90 days, I will pull out my idea folder and go through it, and most of the time, I trash about half of them because once I really look at them outside of that moment of absolute excitement, some do not really appear viable after all. Give your ideas that time to temper; give them time to ferment.

Now take the rest of your viable ideas and categorize them. Do any of them fit into something that you are already doing? Are they good ideas? Next, place them on a priority scale so that you can apportion when you are going to possibly pursue these ideas or if you can pursue them alongside of another idea. You might find that some ideas may not be something that you really want to pursue. Maybe they are important, but they are off track from your true purpose. If so, consider giving those ideas to someone else.

Instead of running from idea to idea and forgetting half of them anyway, pick the best ideas, the ideas that will create the greatest impact in the world, the ones you would actually love to do, and see them through to completion before you move onto the next one.

The next category of entrepreneur is the **Ostrich**. I use the ostrich because any time an ostrich feels threatened, it sticks its head in the sand so it does not have to deal with the outside world or face what is going on around it.

This type of entrepreneur I identified several years back when I was working with craftsmen who later became contractors running their own businesses. The thing is that they love being craftsmen. They love swinging a hammer. Most of these people started out working for someone else, seeing them get the big paycheck and deciding that they wanted to create a business out of this. They love doing it anyway, so they just might as well get the big check. They would create a business around their skill. When they started out, they would normally underbid their jobs. Let's say it was a remodel. They went into somebody's home, they underbid it to make sure they got it because they needed to start their business up, and then they put way too much time into it because they wanted to be "the craftsmen" and do it right. They wanted it to be perfect. But since they underbid it, they could not afford to be a perfectionist. They would get done with the job and wonder why they could not pay off all their debt, why they could not pay their subcontractors, why they could not pay the suppliers for the materials. They were basically out of business before they even got started.

Working with Lightpreneurs™, I have seen this same exact thing. Whether it is EFT, Reiki, Life Coaching or Naturopathic medicine, you love doing what you do so much that you just bury your head in the doing and forget that this is actually a business. Sometimes you forget to charge. Sometimes you forget to market yourself. Sometimes you forget the very things that will allow you to continue doing what you love to do. Once again, I can be guilty of this. I understand. I can empathize with where you are at. It is easy for me to bury my head so deep into helping clients and doing what I love that I forget that I have to look at it as a business to keep the bills paid. This is especially ironic since I am a business coach / consultant and I can forget the very things I am working with clients on.

This one is just as dangerous as the Weather Vane entrepreneur because instead of lacking focus, here you have too much focus and you are focusing on this one little aspect, giving to the people you are trying to help. But at the same time, you are not creating the cash flow. You are not creating the income so you can continue doing this. As you heard me say before, the challenge here is six months later, when you cannot pay the mortgage or keep the lights turned on or put food on the table. You have to go back and get a job, and now you cannot do what you love anymore. You cannot be that practitioner that you are, that artisan, that craftsman, that technician. So once again, success eludes the Lightpreneur™, and you are not able to create the impact you were sent here to create and do what you are supposed to be doing.

The first thing you need to do if you are an Ostrich entrepreneur is to take your head out of the sand and look at how your business makes money and consider other ways that you can provide amazing service and impact to your clients besides the one-on-ones. Ask yourself—what other opportunities would not only create impact, but also generate additional cash flow? We go over this aspect in depth in the "Opening Doors to Your Success" chapter.

The next thing you need to do is at least once a week, sit down and have a meeting with yourself about your business. Create a game plan for what you are going to do that week that includes not only the sessions, but also all the detail work, including keeping up with your client files, bookkeeping, and marketing, as well as looking at other opportunities that will add to your business. By focusing each week on all of these aspects, as well as doing your sessions or other parts of your practice, you will catapult your business much further along.

Lastly, I highly encourage you to have somebody assist you in the business areas you struggle in or just do not like to do. I am a big believer that you cannot afford not to have an assistant. Have somebody come in for just 10 hours a week and pay them $10/hour. Find someone at a local college looking for a part-time job who can help you on the computer or with detail work. Make them part of your weekly meeting to focus on your business and not just your practice.

The third and final category of entrepreneur is the **True Entrepreneur**. There are a few basic things that set the True Entrepreneur apart from the Weather Vane and Ostrich entrepreneurs. The True Entrepreneur looks at what they do as a business first. They know that in order to continue doing what they love, the business has to make money. They have to go out and market and create awareness for what they do so the correct people will come to them, receive the benefit, and then tell other people about it so their business can grow and they can actually do more of what they were called here to do.

Some of the other characteristics of a True Entrepreneur, besides looking at it like a business first, is they ask themselves a few key questions. The first question is **"How does it make money?"** Many people think that is obvious. I trade my service for payment. But let us look deeper into this. For example, a retail store usually does not just sell one particular product. They sell many products that complement and enhance each other. Look at all the different ways your business can make money, not just through the giving of your service. Create an audio file that you can put on a CD, in an email, or have available for download. That audio could be any number of things, for instance, an instructional piece or a tool such as a guided meditation. Creating a journal for them is another product you could consider. We are going to talk about opening additional doors for your client in another chapter. However, I want to let you know that when you get to that chapter, understand that one of the key aspects of a True Entrepreneur is to ask the question, "How does it make money?" and additionally, "What are other ways it can make money?"

Another question a True Entrepreneur asks is **"Will there be enough demand?"** This is not to be negative or say, "Oh, my God, I cannot do this!" but it makes you take a hard look at what you want to do, determine if there is enough demand, and then ask, "How will I be able to expand this to create additional demand?" "How can I market this to create additional awareness, which would then enhance demand?" Be very honest with yourself. If there is not enough demand, maybe you need to look at a different business. Maybe you need to look at a different market or niche. This is a very key question to ask right at the start so you are being honest with yourself and not setting yourself up for failure.

A third question a True Entrepreneur asks is **if someone is successfully doing something similar to this.** This is not to be considered a negative. If no one else is doing it, your job just becomes a bit harder. If you find someone is already doing it successfully, then you should celebrate. Many people become discouraged when they find someone else is already doing something similar to what they are proposing. You should actually be happy because now you know that if someone else can be successful, you can be successful at this, too. An example I use for this is going to the video store. When you go to the video store, look and see if there are any workout videos. Chances are there are plenty in the store. Some people would look at going into that business and say, "There are already so many workout videos. There is no sense in me creating a workout video." That is actually the wrong way to look at it. Celebrate that there are workout videos. Celebrate that there are dozens of abdominal workout videos alone, and that is what you want to create also! If there are that many, obviously, it is an area that you can be successful in. So you take what other people have done, find the ones that are successful, and figure out why they are successful. Copy what makes them successful and put your own spin on it. Put your own branding on it, and you too can be successful because someone else has already blazed the trail. There are people who already want this. There are buyers already in the market calling for this product.

This goes back to the "buyers are buyers are buyers" concept. If someone is a buyer of workout videos, they probably do not have just one. They probably have dozens of them, and the reason they buy additional work-out videos is because they want to see someone else's technique or method. They want to get a different perspective. So how are you going to give them something different? How are you going to give them a new slant in whatever it is that you are doing? Because if there are buyers out there buying something similar to what you have, someone has already been successful in that niche. So find out how they did it, how they became successful, and look at what sets you apart—what makes you unique? Some people may totally resonate with one person and not another, so you are going to have clients who resonate with who you are and what you are doing rather than someone else. They will get more benefit from you, even though you offer very similar information to the other person's. I am a firm believer in "there is no new information." It has all been around for eons. Go back to some of the age-old business concepts. Most of them were written in the early 1900s, and some of the metaphysical concepts were written 2,000-3,000 years ago. But people need *your* interpretation. They need your way of presenting it. You may be the one who triggers what they actually need to receive and how they need to receive it.

The next question the true entrepreneur asks is **"What resources will you need?"** So many people start up a business and do not understand what they are going to need. They run into hurdles right off the bat, and it stops them. I want you to sit down and take a solid inventory of the resources you will need and then, if there are resources you do not have, be creative in the ways you can obtain them. Be creative in the ways you can attract these things to you. Maybe it is having someone mentor you. Maybe it is finding free resources. It could be any number of things, but discover what your needs are going to be and then figure out a way that you can bring those resources in so you can start your business without having to limp from the get-go.

Another question that True Entrepreneurs ask themselves is **"Can I survive the start-up?"** In other words, you need to sit down and look at your finances and really see if you can survive the start-up. In any business you do, there is going to be a start-up. It may even be a very simple business, but most businesses are going to need some amount of time to gain momentum. I try to set everybody up in 90-day cycles because it is a time frame that is not too far out. It is a short enough time span so the end result can be seen, but it is far enough out to give you time to do the things needed to create some foundation so you can actually start off on the right foot and get some traction going on your business.

The final question I would like you to ask is not necessarily what every true entrepreneur would ask themselves, but it is extremely important for Lightpreneurs™. We will say that this is for you to become a True Lightpreneur™. That question is—**"Is this really something that I want to do?"** I know many successful entrepreneurs who have gone out and started a business, and it is not really something they want to do. But they see the business model, they know they can succeed at it, and they have an exit strategy created before they even get started. They are going to sell it off or hire someone to run it. For most Lightpreneurs™, this becomes a very important question. If it's not something you want to do, why are you doing it?

One of my favorite axioms is if you are not having fun, fire yourself and recreate your business so you can have fun. If it is not something you already want to do, how can you make this business something you do want to do? How do you make this business something where you are going to enjoy yourself and be excited to do it? If you dread the day so much that you are constantly hitting the snooze button on the alarm because you want just five more minutes before having to face the day or your job, then maybe you need to rethink what you are doing. I want you to be excited about what you are doing! So excited, you are normally up *before* the alarm clock ever goes off because you are so excited about the day. You are so excited about what you get to do. You are excited about the impact that you are going to create in the world.

So what do you do with all this information? First ask yourself which kind of entrepreneur are you? If you are the Weather Vane entrepreneur, then I want you to create that idea folder and, instead of chasing things constantly and going in different directions, I want you to start focusing on one thing and seeing it through, getting it rolling, and creating some momentum with it before you even think about starting another idea. That does not mean you are not going to have those ideas coming to you, but now you have created a system for those ideas. They get sorted, put into a folder, and looked at on a regular basis, but not too often, so that you can see which ones will actually work in your business model and which ones do not. You may throw a bunch of them away as time goes on, but some of them you will incorporate and, instead of detracting from your momentum, they add to your business and become part of the building process.

If you tend to be the Ostrich entrepreneur, then you have to take your head out of the sand. Yes, you want to do what you want to do—what you are called to do—but you need to look at it as a True Entrepreneur. Hold that meeting once a week to ensure that you are looking at the different aspects of your business, such as opportunities to create additional impact and cash flow and making sure all the details are taken care of. Look at it as a business, not just doing your "practice" or art.

Whether you are the Weather Vane or the Ostrich, either way, you need to stop and first look at it as a True Entrepreneur by looking at what you do as a business first. If it is not generating cash flow for you, then you are not going to be able to do it for long unless you are independently wealthy. Start asking yourself those hard questions. How does it make money? What are other ways it can make money? Is there enough demand? Is someone already successful at it? If so, how can I use their success and do it differently? Put your flavor or spin to it for *your* clients and then ask what resources do I need to get this started? Next, start gathering your resources together and come up with creative ways to have them in place so that when you begin, you already have a solid foundation. Finally, ask yourself if you can survive the start-up financially. Come up with a "worst case scenario" plan so you know what you need to make a go of it and there are few surprises.

Finally, as a True Lightpreneur™, ask yourself if this something you really want to do, and if not, how can you make this into something you want to do? How can you make it fun for you? How can you make it where you are so excited about what you do that you have to do it to feel fulfilled? So now that you are thinking like a True Lightpreneur™, let's move on to the next step.

Chapter 5

Your Key To Success: "Why"

Creating Movement When Faced By the Bear

Are you ready for success? Prosperity? Creating the change that you really want to see in the world? In my experience, there is one key factor that shows whether you are really ready for all of those things. In working with not just Lightpreneurs™, but all types of entrepreneurs, I have discovered that the single biggest indicator about whether that entrepreneur will succeed or not is how big their "Why" is.

> *"In a battle between will and imagination, imagination always wins." --Robert Allen*

What that quote is essentially saying is when push comes to shove, our imagination wins. What we see, the biggest, brightest, and boldest, wins. We can have all the willpower in the world, but in that moment of decision, if our imagination detracts from what we think we want, the imagination is going to win, and it will stop us.

Think of a time when a loved one was late getting home. For most people, we logically think of all the reasons why they could be late getting home. But then the imagination starts to kick in and we imagine all of the crazy things that can be going on, like maybe they were in an accident or doing something they should not be doing. So, in your mind, either they better be dead, or you are going to kill them when they get home. That is, of course, an exaggeration, but it holds different levels of truth depending on the person and the situation. If allowed to run free, our imagination can drive us crazy or work for us to help us achieve our goals.

I believe that everyone has faced some type of difficulty or challenge in their life where in that moment, they did not see how they were going to survive. It might have been in a relationship where someone broke up with us. In that very moment, you don't see how you can survive without that person. Life seems like it just can't go on. It may have been a financial challenge where you were so strapped for money that the bills were much more than the money you had in the bank. You did not know how you were going to survive the week. This was the ruin of you. You were not going to be able to do anything after this. Maybe it was a health challenge. You were facing something, and, many times, even before you go speak to a doctor, you start thinking of the worst. You think, this must be cancer or heart disease, and how am I ever going to survive? In that moment, it is like the big bad bear with nasty, gnarly teeth, and it is coming to eat you. All you can see in your imagination is that bear and how scary and mean it looks and how it is going to simply devour you.

What "Bears" have you faced in your past?

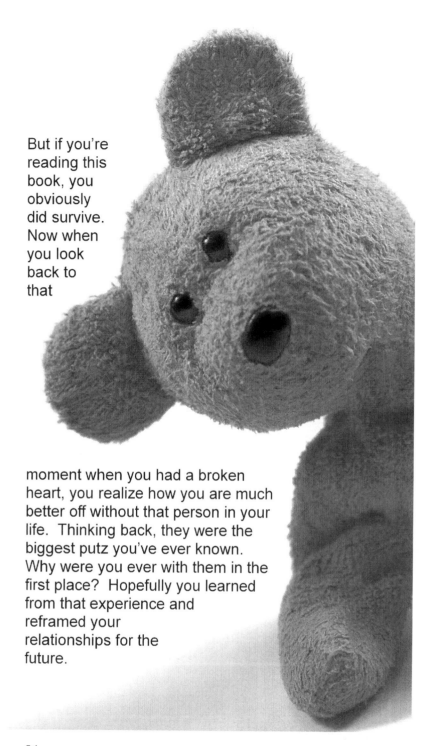

But if you're reading this book, you obviously did survive. Now when you look back to that

moment when you had a broken heart, you realize how you are much better off without that person in your life. Thinking back, they were the biggest putz you've ever known. Why were you ever with them in the first place? Hopefully you learned from that experience and reframed your relationships for the future.

Maybe it was the financial situation and you are reading this book today, so you are surviving. You obviously had food to eat and shelter and, yes, it may have been difficult in that moment, but now looking back, you can garner the lessons from that and move forward with more wisdom and understanding and maybe even with more purpose in your life. If it was the physical challenge, maybe it was the wake-up call for you to start making better choices for your health in diet, exercise, or stress.

So you faced that big, bad bear, and now when you look at it, it is more of a teddy bear. It is something that was painful in the moment, but now when you look back, it may have given you something invaluable to help you make your life better now. I am not trying to make light of those moments, but think of it. When you imagine the worst, it gets the best of you. In those moments If you want to ensure your success as an entrepreneur or Lightpreneur™ of creating the impact that you want to create, I want you to develop the imagination for your *why*. Why are you doing this business? Make it so big, bright, and bold that when the little hiccups do come your way, as they will, your imagination of the end result will be so big that those little things become inconsequential. They are potholes and curves in the road, not brick walls. Yes, they are still there, but your imagination, instead of getting the best of you and leading you to make bad decisions, helps you stay focused on why you are doing this so you can continue to make good decisions. You will look at things with more perspective instead of through distorted lenses.

So what am I talking about here? I am talking about really getting to the root of why you are doing your Lightpreneur™ business. You may have various reasons why you are doing this. I want you to have a primary one. You can have secondary ones also, but I want you to be able to have one so clearly and perfectly defined within you that it is calling you. No matter what tries to distract you or get in your way, you can constantly look at that beacon in the distance and keep moving toward it. That is the key to keep you from getting off track and being stopped instead of keeping you moving toward the success you desire.

Exactly what am I talking about when I say, "your *why*"? Your *why* can be any number of things. For instance, it can be **a cause**. You could be dedicated to the cause of reducing obesity in the world. If this is your cause, I want you to imagine what obesity is doing to people, how it is destroying them, what would be different if people took control of their weight and had a healthy body, and what health means for them physically, mentally, socially, and spiritually. I want you to think that through and create such a bold picture that it is the driving force for you. A cause might be ending war. This example gives me the perfect opportunity to caution you here. I want you to focus on what you want and not necessarily what you don't want. Mother Teresa said it so beautifully. When she was asked to participate in a march against the war, she refused. She told them that when they have a march **for** peace, she would be there. So what are you for? What is your cause? You do need to look at the negative, but not to focus on it. Look at the obesity example and what that is doing to them. What your cause should be focusing on is changing that and the end result. If your cause is eliminating war, know what war is doing to the world and people, but create the picture of what the world will look like when it is filled with peace and love, and make that your focus.

The number and variety of causes that you can have as your *why* is endless. It could be the environment, feeding the hungry, animal rights, or any number of things you are passionate about. There are no limits to the number of causes that you take on, but I cannot stress enough that you make it so bold and vivid in your imagination that you are absolutely compelled to focus your energy on it. It should keep you constantly moving forward and not retreating.

Another example of what can be your *why* is a **belief in what you do**. This can sometimes be confused with the "cause" *why*, but it is actually different. An example of your *why* being a belief is the thought that you can have a new method of using solar power. It can tie into the cause of the environment, but the why here is actually your belief in your *system.* This new methodology is so strong that it goes even deeper than the cause for the environment. Your belief is in the actual process or methodology. It is so strong that that belief is unshakeable. It might be a belief in a methodology or a certain technique you use in your practice. I am not a proponent in there being just one way of doing anything, but if you believe in what you do so strongly, that is a huge *why* because you need to share that with the world. If you have a belief in it, transfer that belief to other people. Let *that* be your *why*. Let that be the flag that carries you through this because you know the power of what you do, and you must share that with the world. A belief in what you do can leave such a strong *why* that it can keep driving you long after most people would have stopped. Look at political campaigns. It is interesting to see that you can have two sides with very different viewpoints. One side has such a belief in their candidate and platform that they cannot even understand how the other side can support the other candidate or platform. It keeps them moving forward no matter what the polls say. They are driven by their belief in their candidate and that candidate's beliefs.

Your *why* could simply be **comfort**. You may be so sick and tired of being sick and tired and so fed up with being broke or whatever you may have experienced that is uncomfortable, that your *why* is comfort. If comfort is your *why*, you need to know exactly what comfort means to you. A lot of people do not even know what comfort would look or feel like. If you have trouble figuring it out, look at what is uncomfortable in your life. Really dig into it and identify exactly what it is and why it is uncomfortable. If the discomfort is that you do not want any more of "x", what would be the opposite of that? What could that encompass? What would the absence of "x" be? What might replace "x" to give you comfort? If you feel discomfort in not knowing how you are going to pay the bills each month, maybe your comfort is knowing the bills are paid easily and freely every month. Your *why* may be creating this business simply to create a level of comfort in your life. If that is your *why*, then once again you need to make it as big and bright and bold as possible to be that driving force and light in the distance that keeps pulling you toward it.

The final *why* I am going to mention here is one that tends to have a lot of both positive and negative energy around it. **Money** is a very interesting why. For a lot of Lightpreneurs™, we think it is wrong to have money as our *why*, as a reason for doing what we love. I have had many clients start one business to generate enough money so they could do what they really want to do. Because of that first success, they then had the ability to go on and do the next thing, which was their real *why*. But the money was important to them to be able to create their true *why*. It gave them freedom, and freedom can be a powerful thing.

A lot of people have an issue with that because they believe that money is "the root of all evil." But it is not. That is not what was actually written in the Bible. People use that so often as the basis or justification for shunning money. It is the love of money, the greed associated with it, having money just for money's sake, as *the* end that is being referred to as evil. If money is your *why*, I encourage you not to have guilt around it. Rather, I challenge you to look just a tad deeper. Look beyond the money. What would money bring to you? It is not really the money you want. I imagine you want money because of what you think money will allow you to have. It might be the one we just talked about: comfort. There is nothing wrong with that. Take it as deep as you possibly can. Many times when I ask people why they really want money, they say they want it to buy a safe, reliable car, a home, or any number of material things. I then ask them to go one step deeper. Why do they want that nice car? It might be that they have driven their car for so long that it is so unreliable that they do not feel comfortable or safe in it, so it is not really the car they want. It is the feeling they are going to get from that new car. The feeling of safety, security, comfort, and freedom. If you want to buy that nice home, why do you want that home? Once again, dig a little bit deeper into the emotional aspects. Is it security, safety, freedom? You can have money as your *why*, but I want you to understand, at a deeper level, the things that you want money to bring to you and the feelings that you want money to bring to you.

If you feel guilty around money, it is probably not wise to use money as your *why*. At the same time, I am going to encourage you not to feel guilty around wanting money. I am, personally, so happy that Bill Gates is one of the richest men in the world because he and his wife set up the Bill And Melinda Gates Foundation. He pledged 35 Billion, with a "B", dollars to start it. Warren Buffet matched that pledge to give that foundation $70 billion+ that is now being used to create amazing change throughout the World. Warren Buffet is now on a mission to work with other wealthy individuals to encourage them to give back the majority of their fortunes to create a positive impact for society. I am so happy that Bill Gates and Warren Buffet accumulated that wealth and prosperity into *their* lives because the world is a better place because of it.

It's amazing when you look back at some of the wealthiest people in the world and how they spent the first portion of their life gathering wealth to them. If they had given it away too early, they might not have been able to create something that has continued on and on. You look at the Carnegie Foundation. Its cause is to promote higher education throughout the world. You look at the Ford Foundation and the impact it has had on the world. On one hand, people can use, as an example, the wealth and excess people live in, but then again, these people give so much of their lives by giving back. Is that the way all of the rich people live? No. But I have a suspicion here that if you have gotten this far in the Calling All Lightpreneurs[TM] book, you will do amazing things when you become successful. You will create amazing change in the world when you have prosperity. This goes hand in hand with honoring the giver. I want you to bring the prosperity to yourself first so you can have the comfort, security, and freedom to do the work you need to do and create an impact. My belief is that if you are a Lightpreneur™, chances are you will use that wealth and prosperity to create a better world, which is the creed of the Lightpreneur™: To make the world a better, brighter place. Who should have the prosperity and the wealth? If not you, then who? Money can be a strong motivator, and it does not need to be evil or a negative thing. It can be an amazing, positive thing. What positive change would you create in the world if you had financial wealth in your life?

So take a moment now to really think about what your *why* truly is because that can be the single biggest thing that drives you to your success. Is your main *why* for doing this because you believe in a cause or because you have such a belief in what you do? Is your main *why* in doing this because you know you deserve to have a certain level of comfort going through this life, or is your *why* money or the things it can bring, not only to you, but also to the world? Once you determine what your *why* is, you need to make it even bigger, brighter, and bolder. How do you do this? You have to be able to experience your *why*; experience the end result of that *why* before it ever actually happens. You need to be able to use all of your senses to create in your imagination the most vivid and real end result that you possibly can.

First I want you to be able to see it. This could be seeing the expression on the face of your clients when they have that major shift. This could be seeing that new home that is going to bring you the comfort and security that you want. This could be seeing that new car or the faces of the children when you have helped supply water to their village. Work with this until you can vividly see the end result of what your *why* is.

Hear it. Hear the voices of the people who have had that shift. Hear the sounds of your new home or even the silence. Listen to the sound of clean water from a well that you have helped a village dig. Laugh over the playful bark of a puppy you have saved from abuse. Imagine the sound of your new car purring like a kitten, completely absent of knocking, grinding, or squealing.

Feel it. Imagine actually touching it and being able to hold it or hug the person. Try to put the sense of touch into it. Feel the textures, the firmness, the temperature. Experience that touch to the deepest level. Take it even further than that.

Smell a scent. Smell the new car odor. Embrace whatever you imagine as part of your why: the wood of a staircase bannister, smoke from the fireplace, the scent of the animals at a rescue shelter, the aroma of food baking in the kitchen of your new home.

Include your sense of taste. Even if it is the feast that celebrates the completion or realization of your cause. The more of your senses that you can involve, the more real it will be to you and the easier it is to keep that at the forefront of your imagination if anything tries to distract or stop you.

I want your *why* to become so real to you that you experience it long before it ever comes to reality. The moment you experience it in your mind, it already is reality. The subconscious cannot discern between imagination and reality. Once you get a taste for it and the experience of it, your subconscious will do everything it can to bring it into your real world, to have it on a regular basis.

If your *why* is a cause, I want you to be able to see the change that happens because of that. If your cause is chasing blight away from the neighborhood, I want you to experience what the neighborhood looks likes when there is no graffiti on the walls and new landscaping has been planted. People feel safe, and there is a connection in the community. I want you to hear the sounds of the children playing in their yards without fear. I want you to smell the people cooking in their backyards because they do not have to be afraid anymore. They have enough prosperity to afford the food to buy and cook. I want you to feel and touch as you imagine hugging the people in the neighborhood who are so grateful because they feel that safety, security, and freedom. I want you to experience this emotionally, so deeply that you cannot believe it has not already happened.

If your *why* is a new home, I want you to imagine that home and use every one of your senses; see it in all its beauty and its safety. Smell the food cooking and see the amazing kitchen where you create healthy meals to feed yourself, your family, and your friends. Hear whatever sounds that bring you comfort there, such as the quietness of a room where you retreat and regenerate. I want you to walk in and feel the fireplace, the wood above it, and the stone around it. Have the sensation of touching it. Go into your office or study and imagine yourself sitting there and how much easier things will come to you and how much you will be able to create and how wonderful it will be to do the work you need and to have a space like that to do it in. I want you to experience it as deeply as possible. An easy way to do this, especially with the home, is to go to an open house. It is amazing how well they are set up to create this sensation for you. Walk in and imagine your own furniture and decorations in this home. Most of the realtors will have something with a good smell in there for you to breathe in and savor the taste. Go in and experience this home for real so you have it embedded in your subconscious to drive you toward that, to give you that end result and keep you motivated when things are demotivating you.

The deeper the experience you have of your *why*, the more real it appears to your subconscious. By doing this, you are giving your subconscious a command to bring this to you. It will constantly be watching for opportunities to fulfill this vision. It will work for your *why*, not against it.

Once there was a traveler who was seeking enlightenment. He came upon the Master and asked if the master could show the way to enlightenment. The master motioned for the traveler to follow as he waded into the river. The master suddenly grabbed the traveler and held his head under water. The traveler struggled and flailed about, fearing for his life. Finally the master pulled the traveler's head up, and the traveler gasped for air. The master then said, "When you want enlightenment as much as you wanted that breath, you will find it." --attributed to The Buddha

There are many variations of this story with "enlightenment" replaced with various other ideas such as: truth, peace, etc. I share this here as another way of looking at your *why* and its importance. When achieving your *why* is as important as that man's breath in that moment, you *will* surely attain it. Nothing will be big enough to stop you. It does not have to be that extreme, but the more hunger you have for its attainment, the more likely you are to realize it. If you truly want something, magnify that hunger. Salivate over its attainment. Want it with every cell of your being, and it will be yours.

So I encourage you, before you go onto the next chapter, to know what your *why* is--a cause or a belief in what you do, comfort, money, whatever it may be. Then I want you to go back and take that *why* and meditate on it for a moment. Put yourself in a quiet place, close your eyes, and imagine the *why* as the end result. In that state of meditation, I want you to experience as fully as possible, with as many of your senses as possible, your *why*. You can even do it as a movie from where it is now to the end result, but I want you to fully embrace it when you get to the end. Embrace that experience and soak it up; drink it in so it becomes a part of you. When challenge comes your way, it will not defeat you because you will have your vision that you truly want, and you will not let *anything* get in your way.

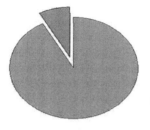

**Creating your
piece of the
pie in a
"down" economy**

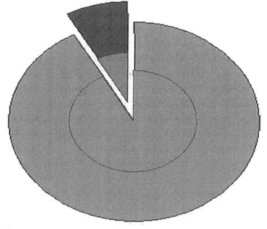

**As the economy grows so
does your piece of the pie**

Chapter 6

A Good Time
To Do Business

The Lightpreneurs™ Wait-loss Plan

I am often asked if a good time to start a business is "now." My answer is that the best time to start a business is always "now," no matter when "now" is, because that is all you have got. The past is already gone, so you cannot go back and start a business. You are not guaranteed another day, so if you do not start it now, when are you going to start it? I know when I am asked this question that people are specifically referring to the supposed bad economic times, and I'd like to address that here.

I believe that the worst time to start a business can be in "boom times." The reason for this is because you are starting a business in a market that cannot sustain itself. Even though we all know you are supposed to buy low and sell high, a buying frenzy can be created during "boom times," and people can start making decisions, not based on true value, but rather on everyone else's buying. Then, all of a sudden, everyone is buying high, and unfortunately most are going to end up selling low because the market will artificially inflate itself so much that it has to come down.

Even though we are experiencing very difficult economic times right now, I believe the downturn in the economy was absolutely necessary in order to clean house. I grew up in a rural area, understanding that occasional forest fires were actually a good thing because they burn out all of the weeds and the brush so that there is a cleansing. It makes way for new and fresh growth to begin. So many businesses over the last several years weren't based on true value to the client. Do we really need a drug store placed on almost every major corner or big box retailers within a block of each other? I do not believe so. There was no real value being added for the customer, so we needed an adjustment in the economy.

An interesting fact is that more than half of the 2009 Fortune 500 Companies and nearly half of the 2008 Inc. list of America's fastest growing companies were launched during a recession or a bear market. So many thriving companies that were started during bad times succeeded because they had to do it right. That is one of the things that starting your business "now" is going to help you focus on—doing business right. Creating the cash flow so you can sustain your business and yourself to keep doing what you are supposed to be doing, your life's purpose, if you will, and offering a true benefit to your clients.

You'll actually be starting your business at a time when the economy has had to reset itself. This is the best time to start a business simply because a lot of the competition has been cleaned out. They were offering hyped-up services with no real value in them. If you start a business now and offer true value to your clients, you can carve out your piece of the pie, and as the economy grows, which of course it will, so too will your piece grow. As I said earlier, it's my belief that we have a limited amount of time to make the choice to create a different world. So I ask you, what are you waiting for? It would be easy for you to use the down economy as justification for procrastination, but the only time you really have is now. If not now, then when? You have clients waiting for you. There are people living in fear and pain. You can help relieve that. Why would you wait? There are many people having a hard time dealing with all of the change. Now is the time for you to step up and help alleviate that. Help people see the light and choose to live in the light and love.

Chapter 7

The Definition of Perfection...

A business that never starts?

Imagine that someone is trying to start a business. They get ready. They start to take aim. They make an adjustment. Maybe they pause to adjust a little more. They go to aim again but the target has moved, so they have to stop and look around for it. They locate it, adjust a little bit, get comfortable with what they are doing, and take aim again. A little more adjusting. It is not quite perfect yet, so they take a couple of steps back and think about what they are aiming at. They take another class on how to aim. They get set up again and try to remember what the target even was. Now too much time has passed, and they have to do something new without ever even pulling the trigger. Does this possibly sound familiar to you? One thing I am constantly telling clients who want to start a business is to not get stuck on having all the details perfected in order to start. Yes, the details are very important to your business. The legal structure and all the other things are vital, but do not forget why you are in business. Remember the goal. Keep your eye on the end result. Start taking action early for the things that are really going to create the success in your business. Thus, the motto to start your business becomes, "Ready, Fire, Aim!"

For most people, that is very out of sync. Many business gurus will tell you to have everything in place before you move forward. But from what I have witnessed with Lightpreneurs™, and even most entrepreneurs, the biggest thing that can stop you from success is your own inaction. In the "Ready, Fire, Aim!" model, what you are doing is getting ready and putting the details together but then, instead of spending all your time trying to figure out everything, you pull the trigger. You see what works and what does not. You adjust the aim and fire again and observe what works and what does not. Readjust your aim with the new information, pull the trigger, and fire again. Then start to aim again, adjust, and repeat. It's the old "plan, do, review" philosophy.

Many Lightpreneurs™ want their business to be absolutely perfect right out of the gate. Is there really any such thing as perfection, or is true perfection actually attainable? What is perfection? This desire, wanting to be absolutely perfect out of the gate, is devastating to many Lightpreneurs™ because by trying for perfection, they do not pull the trigger to start their business. They are waiting for that moment when everything is just right. I would like to share a little story with you around this idea of perfection.

If you will think back to the mid to late 1980s, there was a software program for word processing called Word Perfect. Word Perfect was an amazing program. It was great at what it did. It held the vast majority of the market share for the word processing market. In the mid '80s, a little startup company came along that wanted to have their own word processing program, so they introduced the market to Word for MS-DOS, which later became Word for Windows, the current versions that we know now. When it first came out, it was anything but perfect. I remember having a copy of Word for MS-DOS back in the mid '80s when I was in graduate school. Before I could even finish loading it on the computer, there was already an update, so it was anything but perfect. They had update after update after update. There was Word for MS-DOS 3.0, and then it was 3.01, then 3.02, and they seemed to constantly have new updates. People complained because it was buggy and glitchy and had all these problems. They took all of those problems and worked on them and created something new. Then we would get the next version of Word, and there would be versions .01 and .02 all over again. Then the next version of Word came out, and so on.

Today it is still far from perfect by most people's claims, but because that company was willing to put it out there in all of its imperfection and constantly go through update after update after update, this little startup company is now a mega corporation with the premier word processing program for computers that pulls the greatest market share. Conversely, Word Perfect is difficult to find these days. It is mostly used in a couple of niche markets. It is kind of funny that when I first used Microsoft Word back in the mid-'80s, very few people even knew what it was, and very few people could help me with it because they were using Word Perfect. Now it is very difficult to find anyone using Word Perfect. It's very ironic that the name Word Perfect actually has "perfect" in it. If you are willing to put it out there and change it and allow it to grow by listening to your customers, then you can morph your business into what it's supposed to be and make it the best thing possible rather than waiting for perfection that will never come.

So in relation to your business, if you wait until your business cards are perfect, you are not going to have your cards available to hand out to people as you begin to put the word out there. Just understand that your business cards **are** going to look different in six months. They might even look different in three months. Be OK with that. If you wait for the perfect website, your clients are not going to be seeing you for months and maybe even years. If you are waiting for perfection, it is going to delay you from being able to get the exposure your business needs to get off the ground.

I cannot think of *any* company today that has the same website as they did 5 years ago. Obviously those websites did not start out being perfect. It is going to be an evolution. It's going to change as you go. It is going to change as you learn your customers and your clients better. It is going to change when you know yourself better. The quicker you get over it and just start doing it, adjusting, and modifying as you go, the quicker you will start your business, the quicker you will start figuring out where you actually need to be. As we talked about in the introduction, if you have $50,000 to sink into starting up your business, that is great. Hire a marketing firm, put together an amazing package, and spend tens of thousands of dollars doing it. But I guarantee you even then, six months from now, you will find things that you **could** do differently, that you **should** do differently, that you are **going** to do differently, and even after spending all that money, it is still not going to be perfect.

Speaking of Microsoft, Bill Gates, its founder, has the same 24 hours in every day that you and I do. However, he accomplishes so many things in his 24 hours. He started Microsoft. He, along with his wife, started the Bill and Melinda Gates Foundation. He is involved in a variety of different things, from business, to social events, to philanthropy. How does he do it? Does he just not look at any of the details at all? I doubt that would create the success he has achieved. From what I have learned about him, he looks at the details and then goes with his gut instinct. That is the key to success. Getting the facts and then going with what you feel is right. Whether it is in business, or in law enforcement, or in medicine, you will hear top detectives, top doctors, and top business people talk about how they go with their gut. They go with their instincts.

You, as a Lightpreneur™, need to learn to trust that skill of going with your gut. Most of you reading this book know this. You understand intuition. You understand guidance. But so many of us, when we get into business mode, forget all of that. I want to encourage you to lower your thinking 12 inches. What I mean by that is get out of your head. Start "feeling" what the answer is in your heart. Being stuck in your head will give you paralysis by analysis. You are going to spend so much time sorting through the details, then re-sorting through them and looking at them in another way, then another way, that you may never create the action to move your business forward and give you a chance at success. So lower your thinking and get down into your heart. Feel what is right once you have the facts. Do not allow your mind to cloud what your truth is.

I highly suggest you use some form of kinesiology to help you make better, faster decisions. For those of you who are not familiar with kinesiology, let me give you a little point of reference. There are several methods, however the easiest is likely the "stand strong" method. It takes two people to use this method, but it is dramatic, which helps if you are not familiar with kinesiology. In this method, have one person stand comfortably with feet shoulder width apart. Have them take several deep breaths. They should focus on their breathing to clear any thoughts or energy. It is also important for the person doing the testing to clear their thoughts and energy. Determine the dominant hand of the person being tested. The person doing the testing should stand facing the subject, a little offset to the subject's dominant side. Once both subject and tester are relaxed, centered, and focused, ask the subject to raise their dominant arm straight out from the side. Present a question or object to the subject and ask them to resist as hard as they can as you try to push their arm down using the index and forefingers.

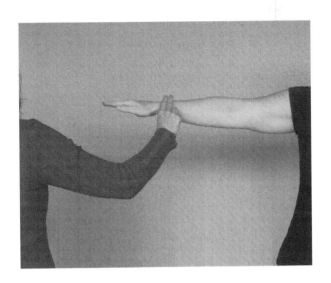

An easy start is to ask them to say their name out loud: "My name is _____." Have them hold strong and then try to push their arm down using two fingers. You will notice you cannot push their arm down. Next, have them relax and repeat the process, but give them another name to say instead of their own. For example, if their name is Carol, have them say out loud, "My name is

Michael" while trying to resist again as you are pressing down on their arm. Most people are shocked that when they say their real name they can easily resist, but when they say something that is not true, they are powerless to resist your fingers pushing down. Now play with this with other "truths," and you will be amazed. If you encounter a "false positive" or "false negative," look at the energy around everything involved: the subject, the tester, the question, etc. Keep the questions very simple so there is less possibility for truth and untruth to exist in the same moment.

You can also use this method to test what foods are good for you by holding them against your chest with your non-dominant hand as you do the test. Once you have mastered the technique, you can use it to discover the "truth." Just remember to keep it clear and simple. If needed, break the question down into smaller components so one "false" aspect does not throw off the entire answer. I have experimented with kinesiology extensively. I use it to help guide me, whether it is what I should eat, a business venture, or anything else. I listen to my body. I lower my thinking 12 inches and essentially get out of my mind and listen to my heart or, in this example, my body. I go with my feelings. I go with my gut.

This is all in alignment with the "if you are not having fun, fire yourself" ideology mentioned in other parts of the book. Your mind can create something for you that sounds really good from an intellectual standpoint, but when you get into the doing aspect, it is not something you really enjoy after all. It is not something you want to do. It is not something that excites you in the morning when you get up. If you **listen** to your body, you are going to enjoy what you do and it will not be such a struggle. So get the facts, sort them out, and use whatever method you need in order to look at them objectively, find your truth, listen to your heart, and let the final decision be from your gut.

I believe one thing that really holds people back is when they have gotten to the point where they cannot make decisions. They are inundated with so much information coming from every direction that they do not want to make decisions anymore. If you want proof of this, go into a fast food restaurant and just hang out for a while. It is amazing to watch people looking at the board, not able to make a simple decision of what *feels* right for them to eat. They go through this mental process trying to figure it out. If they truly felt what was right for them, they would know what to order for their body because their body would tell them. The interesting side note to this is that we are being polluted by too much advertising today. We are inundated constantly with advertising companies telling us what we should want. If we just listen to ourselves on a daily basis, we would know to slow down. We would know to remove some of the stress. We would know to do the things that feel right and experience much more happiness as a result.

Applying this back to your business, do the things that need to be done to get the business moving forward, but do not get hung up on trying to figure out every single detail. The result of allowing yourself to get bogged down with the details could result in having to go back and get that job you hate because you have not even been able to get your business started. Stop spending so much time analyzing what you are going to do and instead, just put it out there and then get feedback from your customers.

We are going to go into detail on this in the "Systemize for Success" chapter. For now I want you to realize that if you listen, your clients will tell you what products and services you should be offering or about the changes you should be making in your current products and services. They will tell you how to market to them. They will tell you how to create a business that they will want to do business with. Once again, get out of your head because what they are telling you may not make sense, but sometimes you just have to do it anyway and trust the process.

Start today trusting yourself. Start giving yourself credit for the amazing being that you are. You either have the information, or you can easily find it. Today with the internet, information is so readily available to help you move forward in your business. It is all there. One way you can get support is through social networking. It's not about creating virtual farms or aquariums or lives on the internet, but really making connections with people who want to help. The answers are everywhere if you will just listen.

As a Lightpreneur™, you know how to access the source. You just have to be willing to tap into it. If you are willing to breathe deeply, lower your thinking 12 inches, and then start connecting with that true source, you can have the answer any time you want it.

So ask yourself: what are the things you are waiting on right now? What are the things you have not pulled the trigger on that you have been aiming at for quite some time? Think of one thing that you have been holding off on that you can start in the next week, two weeks, or a month at most. Something that you are going to create, and do that one action item to start. If you have been in business for a while, what is that thing that has needed to change for a while but that you have not been willing to go back and adjust? What is one thing that is working well that you can decide to do more of? What is the next version of your product or business? Quit waiting for perfection, put it out there, and start developing what your clients really want. Are you ready to GO? Are you willing to aim, pull the trigger, and create the impact you came here to create? If so, let's go create a business.

Chapter 8

Getting "Nichey"
Finding the rhythm

I am a firm believer that when you target a smaller niche with your service, your potential market actually becomes bigger. Discovering what your true niche is and starting to identify who your ideal clients are can actually be one of the biggest booms for your business. It can also magnify the impact that you create for your clients. One thing I have discovered with Lightpreneurs ™ is that those who try to serve everyone usually end up serving no one or, at most, a very few. The main reason for this is that their message is so broad and so generalized that no one really hears it. The more you narrow your niche, the better you are able to speak in the vocabulary of your ideal client, and they will be more apt to hear it. The other reason I believe that practitioners who go after everyone in the market end up with fewer clients is that they are coming at it from a *lack* mentality rather than an abundance mentality, and that needy energy does not work to attract new clients.

In order to start identifying what your niche is, we first need to define what a *true client* is. I am going to be addressing more about a concept that I refer to as the ideal client later. What I refer to as a true client and an ideal client are not the same. Keep in mind that it is best if your ideal client is also a true client. *A true client is simply one that works for your business model.*

A true client has three characteristics. The first characteristic is that they need what you have to offer. This seems a bit obvious at first. Of course your true client has a need for what you offer. But many times we pursue clients that do not really need what we have to offer. It sounds good. It may be trendy to have a psychic or a life coach, but the question is, are they coming to you out of true need, or a desire to have what someone else has at this moment? If someone does not really have a true need, are they really serving your purpose of making the world a better, brighter place, or are you just doing your service just to do it? I really want you to look at each client and see if they truly have a need for what you have to offer. Most of them will. I just do not want you spending time going after clients who do not have a real need for what you have to offer. Taking on clients without a real need is a very short term strategy for business because they will not be the ones who are the missionaries for your business, going out and telling everybody about its amazing impact. Once the fad aspect has gone away, so will they, and they will not have brought you any additional clients. So you are out there marketing all over again, just as hard as you did from the start. You may even have to market harder and spend more time now because you were marketing to a target client that really did not have a true need for your services to begin with.

The next characteristic a true client should have is *want*. Again, this one seems simplistic, but I see so many practitioners chasing people who do not want what they have to offer and trying to convince people that what they have is something they really need.

> "A man convinced against his will, is of the same opinion still." --Bryan Tracy

So yes, you may be able to convince some people, especially short term, that they need your service. But I can guarantee that there are clientele out there that already want what you have. You do not have to be in the convincing or sales business. I am not talking here about educating the public. I want you to go out and be the educator, but do not try to convince someone whom you just educated how much they need you. If they do not get it, allow them to go on their journey and then put your focus on the people who do get it. Remember, it will be much easier for you to focus your energy on people you can truly help. It comes down to the 80/20 rule or the Pareto Principle which we will talk about in detail in chapter 11. Twenty percent of the people are going to get it and want it. Focus on them and do not chase after the eighty percent who do not want or get it. You are going to have a much happier life if you concentrate your energy on the ones who absolutely want and are excited about what you have to offer.

The final characteristic of a true client is someone who has *the ability to pay*. For some of you, this is going to ruffle your feathers because you want to service people even if they do not have the ability to pay. That is fine, but they should not be part of your business model as a true client. They should be seen as a means of giving back and tithing to your community. If you put these people in your business model as your true clients, as part of your cash flow, you'll starve. The clients who do not pay will come to you without giving, and you are going to give and give and give and not receive anything in return. It goes back to honoring the giver. There are people out there who will take from you without giving, and that is not respecting you or your gift or the whole process. Yes, there are going to be people out there who have a true need for what you have to offer and they are going to have the want and the desire for it, but they are not going to have the ability to pay. Just do not include them in your business model as part of what is generating your income for you to sustain your business. Put those people in your business model as your tithing, your giving back. Focus your marketing efforts on the ones who have the need, the want, and the ability to pay.

Now let's jump into my concept of the ideal client. What exactly is an ideal client? When I was working toward my MBA, they taught us about demographics, age, income ranges, and knowing your demographic. I am going to actually ask you to take it one step further by having you identify an *ideal* client. It does not matter if it is someone who is real or imagined. I want you to be able to put a face to this client. I want you to be able to put energy on this client. When you come up with this person who is your ideal client, they are essentially going to be the average of the demographic. So if your demographic is between 35-45 years old, they are probably going to be 40 years old. If your demographic has an income from range from $35,000 - $55,000, their income is probably going to be $45,000. The reason I want you to come up with one person is that you can get inside of one person's head. Those of you who are involved in hypnotherapy or guided imagery in some way can actually put yourself in a trance state to feel this person and get to know them. We are doing this so you will understand better how to reach them and let them know that what you have to offer will benefit them. You will know how to share with them the information you have so they understand what you offer and want it. I want you to get detailed and pick a specific gender, age, career, and what types of interests and hobbies they have because now you can get inside this person's head, imaginary or real, and figure out how you should speak to them, what words will be best at conveying your information specifically to them. You can ask yourself how to recognize who they are. What are some of their biggest challenges that you can help them overcome?

As you are coming up with this ideal client, there are three main concepts that I want you to look at. The first one is: *who can truly benefit the most from what you offer?* Like I mentioned earlier in the chapter, nearly anyone can benefit from what you do, but who can benefit the absolute most? I want you to be really honest with yourself around this. Is it someone who has a certain type of health issue? Is it someone who had a specific type of challenge in their life? Is it someone who belongs to a certain category or group? What is the characteristic that stands out so that when you work with someone with this characteristic, you get "Wow!" results? Anytime I work with someone like that, they have immediate results. Once again, if you focus on this, you are going to spend less energy and resources and create a greater impact with your client and in the world. You will have so much more joy within yourself knowing that you are doing what you came here to do.

The second thing I would like you to look deeply at as you are trying to discover your ideal client is: *who can you benefit with the least effort?* This goes back to using your resources wisely. Your most valuable resource is time. You can buy or attract more of any other resource into your life, but once time is used, it is gone forever. Use this resource especially wisely. You may be able to create a great impact for one particular person, but if you are spending all your time doing it, maybe that is not who your ideal client is. You might be able to create just a slightly smaller degree of impact for another person but use one tenth of the time. Now you can expand what you do times ten. Another valuable resource for most Lightpreneurs™ is energy. We all know those people who drain our energy. How many clients can you work with who totally drain your energy? Can you work with clients who actually *give* you energy? Would that expand your ability to create impact in the world? There is only so much of "you" to go around. Use yourself and your personal and business resources wisely. Again, who can you benefit with the least effort?

The final element I want you to embrace as you are developing the concept of your ideal client is determining *what type of client you are happiest working with.* My axiom here is if you are not having fun, fire yourself and start over. If you are working with clients who do not make you happy, are you going to be any happier three or four years from now? Are you going to give up because you are just not having joy in your life? The Giver of your gift meant for you to have joy and a fulfilling life, which includes who you work with. Who, as a client, brings you the most joy? Think about when you see that change or shift and you know they get it, which makes your heart sing and your soul jump for joy.

Drill down and identify specific attributes of this person. Use these three characteristics to start determining who your ideal client is. Be very specific, picture them, and put yourself in their thoughts and think how they think. Imagine yourself going through their day so you can find opportunities to present what you have to offer to them and show how it can benefit them.

I want to leave you with one last aspect when you are thinking about a niche. Many of you have already struggled with knowing what you want to focus on as a niche. I am going to give you a suggestion that helps many of my clients. Think of life as climbing up a mountain. There are going to be areas when everything is going good, and then there are going to be areas where it is very difficult. I want you to imagine the times in your life when you have felt that you were lost in a dark valley and you could not seem to find your way. You may have felt hopeless and defeated. I call this "being in the valley of the shadow." I can almost guarantee that everyone reading this book can remember a time in their life when they were going through that. I want you to look back at your valley of the shadow, look at where you were when you were going through it and who you were, and ask yourself, knowing what you know now, what would you be able to do for someone who is currently going through that? I think you will find amazing things that you can offer after having gone through and survived that experience.

Let me give you a little caveat here. If you are currently in the middle of a valley of the shadow, that is not the niche I am talking about. This is one that you are on the other side of. It's one you went through some time ago and learned important life lessons from. If you are still in it, I am not suggesting you use that as your niche. Rather, a valley that you have come through gives you the ability to help someone who has not made it through that valley yet. Because you have been through your valley of the shadow, you can empathize with people who are going through that same experience. You understand what they are facing. You understand what they are feeling. You understand the journey that they are going through.

Imagine for a moment that you are sitting in a class where the topic is drinking and driving. You were sent there by the court as a mandatory part of your punishment for a DUI offense. You are listening to the presenter talk about all the reasons why you should not drink and drive and why alcohol is bad. Someone asks the presenter, "What is your experience with alcohol?" Imagine the response is, "I would never drink. It is evil, it is a sin, and I have never touched alcohol in my life!" Where does the respect from the students in that room go in that moment? It is definitely not with the presenter because they do not feel the presenter can relate to their experiences.

This is an extreme example, but it shows how important it can be to relate to people going through a specific situation. If you have been through the valley of the shadow that your potential clients are going through, you will garner greater respect for having traveled that same path. You will be able to reach them in a way that someone who has not experienced their journey could ever do. You will be able to say things to them that someone who has never been there would never be able to say. This gives you a rapport with that type of client that someone else would never be able to achieve.

Now if you have identified your valley of the shadow, I encourage you to further educate yourself and learn more about the process of what you have gone through so that you not only have the experience to speak from, but you also have the expertise.

I would like to share something with you that goes hand in hand with this. There are three types of knowledge.

The first type is learned knowledge. Reading this book is a form of learned knowledge. Going to a class and hearing an instructor is learned knowledge. Learned knowledge is good, but I believe most people will agree that it is not the most effective form of knowledge and does not give us actual *skill*. I can read for a lifetime about how to paint a masterpiece, but until I pick up a brush and take that first stroke across the canvas, it does not mean nearly as much as having the brush in my hand applying paint to canvas. Now the teaching begins to make more sense, and I gain a deeper understanding.

This leads us to the second form of knowledge: experiential knowledge. In my experience, there is nothing like experiential knowledge. It is one thing to read about something in a class room; it is quite another to experience it and go out and do it. But combining learned knowledge with experiential knowledge adds to both. This is a situation where one plus one does not equal two, but rather, equals 11. It is exponentially more powerful than either one alone. Using the painting analogy, I can have some knowledge from learned knowledge and some from experiential knowledge, but the moment I put those two together, the understanding and the ability is magnified so greatly that it makes me that much more capable of painting.

The third type of knowledge is teaching knowledge. Teaching knowledge is absolutely amazing. You actually receive knowledge from teaching a subject because you have to understand the concepts at a much deeper level, and your understanding gets deeper by the mere preparation of teaching. Most good teachers I know learn more from their students than they actually teach to the students. That is the sign of a good teacher: one who continues to grow in their subject because they are constantly learning. Getting questions from their students makes them learn and grow even more. It takes their knowledge to a whole new level, leading to wisdom. Now let us add experiential knowledge, learned knowledge, and teaching knowledge together. It is one plus one plus one, which equals 111. You have just taken another exponential jump. So any one of these by themselves is not very strong. Individually they can actually be quite weak. When you combine all three, they magnify the magic of each other and start creating wisdom for you on a whole new level.

We all know people who have gone to school, learned something, and ended up with little to no actual knowledge around the subject. We know people who have gone around the block experientially a few times, and they still are learning the same lesson over and over again. Most of you, I am sure, have had teachers who teach the concepts, yet they did not understand the truth about the subject they are involved in or how it applies in the "real world." I am encouraging you to consider your niche as something you have gone through and then start to explore more from a learning state. Combine that experiential knowledge with the learning, and then go out and start teaching. You will become so wise in your niche that you will have many clients seeking you out. This is just a suggestion and only one of many ways to determine your niche, but one that many Lightpreneurs™ specifically have used to discover how to harness their purpose to its greatest end.

I would just like to reiterate that the more you are willing to let go of **everyone** being your client and define your true niche, the more you can serve at a higher level without expending a lot of energy and resources. If you do that, you will create a Lightpreneur™ business that will amaze you and be of enormous benefit to the world.

Chapter 9

Uniquely You
Standing out from the herd

What makes you "uniquely you" or more importantly, what makes your business unique amongst all the other businesses out there? We've all heard the phrase, "standing out from the herd." In business, this is absolutely important because if you are just another sheep in the herd, you will be skipped over and just lumped in with the rest. But then there is the black sheep that stands out from the herd. That is the one you can spot a mile away. Even though we think in negative terms about black sheep, everybody notices them. They are the ones who get talked about. That is what you want for your business. You want to stand out and have people notice and talk about you. That is an amazing thing for business, and you need that to happen for your Lightpreneur™ business.

In the business world, this is actually called a USP or Unique Selling Proposition. Your USP is what makes your company, product, or service stand out from all the others. The worst thing in the world is to be another "me too!" in whatever business you are in. Whether it's hypnosis, life coaching, or interior design, if you are just another one of those businesses, it's going to be hard for you to survive because what differentiates you from everybody else? What's going to let them know that you are special or unique? Being unique does not necessarily mean that you are the best or the worst; it's just different. It's something to separate you and make people take notice.

What are some of the categories to separate you? It can be your business name. We are going to get off the main focus of the chapter for a moment here to make a very important point. What does the name Starbucks have to do with coffee? How about Target with a department store? Apple with computers? Google with searching or finding information? What does Hertz have to do with rental cars? Maybelline with cosmetics? I think you get the idea. These are all companies at the top of their industries, but their names have nothing to do with what they actually do.

It is much more important for your business name to be memorable rather than descriptive. Many Lightpreneurs™ get hung up on creating the "perfect name" that absolutely describes their business. There are countless incidences of Lightpreneur™ businesses being stalled for months trying to discover the "perfect" name. I have seen crazy, long names for Lightpreneur™ businesses in an attempt for them to let everyone know EXACTLY what they do. The result is a name so long that it is difficult to remember, impossible to enter as a web address without making a mistake, and more like a tag line than a name. Lightpreneurs™ itself is a unique name that people have to stop and process and then talk about.

Notice that Lightpreneurs™ is a made up word, and most people do not have a clue what it really means. When I use the term Lightpreneurs™, it's not a name that gives everyone the absolute description of what I do, but my clientele get it. They do not need the name to describe exactly what I do because they just get it. Let's look at a few other business names. What does Ford have to with cars? Hewlett Packard with computers? Mary Kay with cosmetics? Disney with entertainment? In all of these, the company name is the founder's name. I would offer that one of the best ways to create your USP or brand your business today is self-branding. For many of you, your brand could and should be your own name. It is simple, easy, and can create not just an identity for your company, but personality and character also.

Your USP surely does not have to be your name. It could be a logo. For example, if you have children and they are like most kids, they can spot the McDonald's golden arches from miles away and will start begging you to stop before you even get close. This is a unique logo that is so identifiable, people unconsciously recognize it and have an emotional response to it without even seeing the name. It could be your slogan. Nike's "Just Do It" has become so popular and so famous that it's used in all different categories of life, but we still associate it with Nike. It could be your pricing. I remember when I first heard about Starbucks. The reason people were talking about it was the price. I asked myself, "Why are people going over there and paying so much money for a cup of coffee?" I had to go into a Starbucks and buy a cup just to find out why people were paying $4 for a cup of coffee. Now I meet clients in Starbucks all over the country. You may think that you cannot create a brand or a name, like a large corporation, to create uniqueness, but it only has to appeal to your actual market.

There are an unlimited number of areas that may be easier (and less expensive) that you can use to create uniqueness for you and your business. It may be that how you deliver your services to your clients is so different from similar businesses that it makes your business stand out. I've known many professional speakers who use the way they dress as their USP or what makes them stand apart from everyone else. By narrowing your niche down, you can become unique in whom you actually target because no one else serves that particular group of people. It's just like the song in the movie *Fame*, you want them to "remember your name," remember you, and remember your business. All you have to do is create that recognition and uniqueness so that your ideal client will get and understand and recognize you and see you as separate from all the other businesses that are similar to yours.

When we are talking about USPs, I want you to see a bigger picture. Your USP should offer something that is going to create buzz and have people talking about you, your business, and what you do. Having a great USP is not about being the best, but rather about being unique and standing out. A good exercise to help you with this is to think of businesses or people you know that are very successful and ask yourself what sets them apart. What makes them stand out from everyone else? Do they have the best burger? Well, McDonalds is the most successful burger chain right now, and I think most of us can agree that they do not have the absolute best burger out there. I believe they are one of the biggest fast food chains because they offer consistency. You basically know what you are going to get whether you are in L.A. (Los Angeles) or LA (Louisiana). Over the last several years, Starbucks has been the most successful coffee shop in the world, and tests have suggested that they do not have the best coffee. I believe it is the environment they create. So being "the best" isn't necessarily the easiest way of setting yourself apart. Creating uniqueness around what your customers experience emotionally in a positive way when they think about your business is what really matters. Look at some of the businesses you frequent. Look at some of the other Lightpreneur™ businesses that you enjoy or respect, and find out what sets them apart. Sometimes it can be very minor things that we do not really think of as setting someone apart, but when we look deeper, it is something that really creates the difference.

Chapter 10

Marco... Polo
Helping your clients find you

Have you ever played Marco Polo while swimming? One person closes their eyes while everyone else swims around trying not to get tagged. The swimmer who is "it" calls out "Marco," and the other swimmers call back "Polo." Marco then uses the sound to try to find the other swimmers to tag. You should not have your clients blindly trying to seek out you and your business. You should do everything you can to help them find you and what you have to offer. You may think you are in the Life Coaching or Hypnotherapy or Energy Worker or Medicine or any of a variety of those types of businesses, but that is not your business at all. First and foremost, your real business is marketing. No matter how great a practitioner you are, it will not matter if people do not know what you do and how it will benefit them. The primary business you are in is marketing your business or creating awareness for the benefit you offer your potential clients/customers. Many Lightpreneurs™ have a challenge with the term marketing simply because it is a business term, and they have a deep aversion to "business." I am going to recommend that you forget about the word marketing and just think of "creating awareness" because creating awareness truly is what marketing is all about for a Lightpreneur™.

Marketing is usually broken down into the four P's: Product, Place, Price, and Promotion, which are all major components of the marketing process, but the real key is creating awareness. There have been many textbooks written on marketing, so in a single chapter, I cannot go over everything there is to know about marketing. It would take an entire book just to cover the 4 P's to any real degree. But, what I will do here is to give you in a nutshell what I think are some of the most important aspects for a Lightpreneur™ business.

Product:

The first P in the four P's is Product. Product also includes services. Many Lightpreneurs™ are primarily in a service business. After reading the "Opening Doors to Your Success" chapter later in the book, you will probably begin to realize how you can expand your practice and your impact by opening additional doors for your current and potential clients.

In our discussion of products and services, I ask people to tell me what they offer. They will usually give me some explanation of their tools, gifts, and modalities—all of the things they do—when they should be telling me what the end result of what they do is. Zig Ziglar, many decades ago, talked about this concept in an analogy by saying do not sell drill bits, sell holes (or for our purposes, the (w)hole of something). What he was trying to convey is that most people do not really want drill bits. What they really care about is the end result, the hole. They want to know that by using this product, it will create a hole quickly, easily, smoothly, and be able to create many holes. The drill bit is simply the means to get what they really want.

But most people when they try to sell drill bits focus on the drill bit and not the end result: the hole. They will tell us that it is titanium steel 135 degree split point. That is not what we actually want. It may be what helps create the end result, but the end result is not what is being focused on. As a Lightpreneur™, you may want to talk about all the great gifts, tools, and talents that you have and use. But it is what those create for the client that the client wants to hear about.

What is the (w)hole that your business creates? What problem do you solve for the client? What is the client going to experience as a result of working with you? What will they receive by engaging in your service? What is the end result the client will receive from your Lightpreneur™ business? That is where you want to focus because all these details are what they are listening for. Everyone is tuned to their own favorite radio station, *WIIFM*: What's In It For Me? We will use a 30-second commercial as an example.

A 30-second commercial is one of the most important marketing pieces you can create for your business. If you can convey in an interesting, captivating way what your business does in 30 seconds or less, you can create your website, your brochures, and all of your marketing pieces from the basic information in that commercial. Once you get the essence of your business to fit into 30 seconds that leave people listening and wanting to know more, you have the basis that you can expand into any vehicle you might want to use in creating awareness for you and what you do.

Following are two different 30-second commercials as an example of just how key this really is. Read them both out loud so you can get the full impact of what is being shared with you. Here is the first one:

The standard 30-second commercial

"Hi! My name is Elmas Vincent with Diamond Life Creators, and I am a life coach and an NLP, or Neuro-linguistic Programing practitioner. As a life coach, I help people determine what their goals and dreams are and then work with them to create a game plan on how to get there. Finally, I hold them accountable so they can realize those goals and dreams. With the NLP we can remove blocks and fears. So whatever you would like to see bigger, brighter, and better in your life, I can help you with that. By using different coaching models and asking powerful questions, I will help you discover what you really want in life and how to get there. I will be at the back of the room with my business cards where we can talk about how my coaching and NLP can help you."

If you have attended any networking events, you have probably heard something very similar to the first example. Now let's look at a second example. Read this out loud so you can see how it impacts you.

The alternative 30-second commercial

"Have you ever wanted to start your own business and you just didn't know where to begin? You are working at your job, and you feel like your life is just slipping away because you know that you are here for a purpose. But what is that purpose? Each morning you keep hitting the snooze button because you just don't want to face another day. Well, at Lightpreneurs™, we help you discover what your true purpose is and then help you create a plan on how to turn your purpose into a viable, prosperous business that will create an impact in the world. We will work with you on that plan to help you transition from that J-O-B to what you were meant to be doing. We will help you get to where you are so excited about each new day that you can't wait to get up. My name is Elmas with Lightpreneurs™, and I will be at the back of the room to talk to you about how to start living your life of purpose."

So what was the difference between the two? Did the first one really affect you? Did it have an emotional impact on you? For most people it does not because it is all about ME, Elmas, the life coach. How great I am and all the tools I have and what I do. It is not focused on the client, so they are not hearing it. The first one starts out with my name and my business name. I will be blunt here. They do not care. They are listening for how it will help them and what the benefit is, and you filled the first part of it with your information. You have lost their attention right at the start. Notice how much the word "I" is used in the first example. In the second example it is all about the potential client, "You," and it talks about how "we" will be doing this.

With all the information we are bombarded with every day and all the mind chatter that everyone is listening to, you have at most ten seconds to capture their attention. If it is all about you in the first ten seconds, you have lost them. They are already thinking about other things that are going on in their lives. You need to use the first ten seconds to talk about them and what's going on in their life and how you can benefit them. If instead you *start your thirty-second commercial or any of your marketing pieces with a powerful question or a bold statement,* you begin to captivate them. Those are the types of starts that interrupt their mind chatter and get them to pay attention to what you are saying. Try this for yourself. When you are talking with a group of people, suddenly ask a question and watch what happens. Most people will shift instantly and start paying attention, even if they were only half listening before. This is because we are trained to listen for questions because we might need to provide an answer. Think back to when you were young and your parent or teacher suddenly asked you a question and you were not paying attention. Those old emotional anchors are in almost everyone, commanding them to instantly pay attention. When we hear someone make a bold statement, it brings up the challenge aspect in us. "Oh yea, prove it!"

In the alternative 30-second commercial, I do not mention that I am a Life Coach or NLP practitioner or speak about the tools I use. It is all about the client. I can guarantee you I get much more response from the second version than from the first.

The other thing Lightpreneurs™ tend to do is talk in what I term "high vibrational vocabulary." We talk about manifesting, law of attraction, positive affirmations, and energy. If your client is vibrating at a lower level, they tend to not be able to hear you when you use the high vibrational vocabulary. You need to start where they are at; at their vibrational level. If they are struggling with finances, you need to start where they are vibrating at in that struggle and then show them there is a better way and that you know the path to that way. That is what they will understand. You start out speaking in their vocabulary, where they are at right now, and then give them a glimpse of what they can attain.

Most people think they are very logical. They think they make buying and other decisions based on the facts and reason. What I would like for you to understand is that almost everyone actually buys based on emotion. So you need to talk to them emotionally. Look at some of the things you and people you know have bought in the past which ended up only being used a couple of times and then retired to a closet or the garage. We buy those items because in the moment we have an emotional attachment to them. We do not feel like we can do without them. But once we get them home, they become more of a burden and in the way than actually useful. People buy on emotion, and then they justify their decisions with logic.

Look over your marketing pieces; review your 30 second commercial and ask yourself, does this create an emotional response or is this just words? Are your words there to impress people with who and what you are or to really share how you are there to serve them? Do you have alphabet soup that looks good to you behind your name (ie: cht, lmt, etc.) or do you have information that speaks directly to the client in a way that makes them want to move and create action around what you are offering to them?

Place:

The next of the four P's is place. It is also referred to as distribution. Place typically includes many different aspects when talking about pure marketing, including: inventory, transportation, storage, distribution, etc. For our purposes here we are going to focus on where you actually put yourself, your services, and your products to be in front of potential customers. We live in a very different age, and the place option is expanding every day. One of the biggest places that you can offer your service now is on the Internet. You may offer your service via a video channel such as Skype or a recording or text file as a download. When you read the "Opening Doors to Your Success" chapter, you should see many different opportunities to expand the places that you offer your business and impact to the world.

Place is a very important part of the 4 P's. As a Lightpreneur™, you should determine who your "ideal client" is and how to get what you have that will impact them in front of them. Once you know more about who you client is, it is easier to know where to place your business physically and virtually to create the greatest opportunities for your client to find and experience the benefit you bring.

Price:

The third P is price. Price is an extremely important part of your marketing mix. If it's too high, it can create a barrier for your clients to even discover you. If it's too low, your services can be seen as inferior or cheap. Cheap in this context is not a positive. There is a big difference between cheap and inexpensive. That difference usually lies in perception. You may be the best at what you do, but if you offer your services at too low of a price, your clients may question why it is really so low. Most people have a belief that "you get what you pay for." In creating your marketing strategy, you need to look at the entire picture.

There are a variety of different pricing strategies. The one strategy I would encourage you to avoid is the *low price strategy* because most people equate low price with low quality. I want to encourage you to honor and respect the value that you bring to the world because if you do not honor and respect it, neither will your clients.

106

As an example, let's say the low end is Wal-Mart, and it goes all the way up to a store such as Nordstrom. Wal-Mart markets itself as the low price leader, and Nordstrom markets itself on quality and outstanding customer service. I am not suggesting that you price yourself like Nordstrom on the extreme high end, however, the higher end is a better place to compete for Lightpreneurs™, in my opinion. If you try to compete on a price, someone can always come in at a slightly lower price, and if a low price is what your customer is truly looking for, your competitor can take away your customers. I would rather see you create customer loyalty based on the quality and impact that your services create, not simply because it is the cheapest thing people can find. Cheap can always be beaten by cheaper. Quality is always quality. Results are results. Actually, I would encourage you to have a full range of prices. You will read a great deal more about this in the "Opening Doors to Your Success" chapter.

Another aspect under price is packages. This is not referring to how you package your products physically, but rather bundling what you have and then offering the bundle at a less expensive price than the items would be individually. For example, you could offer six coaching sessions, four follow-up emails, an all-day class, and a journal. If these were purchased individually, they might be $900. But you might offer them as a package for $600. This benefits both you and the client. If they take the class, then it makes your job in the coaching sessions easier and more impactful. The journal gives you material to use in the sessions that, again, makes your coaching easier and more impactful. The client may have an easier decision in deciding to do what will create the greatest benefit for her. You can increase your total income easier by clients purchasing more services up front, which frees you from having to spend additional time and resources marketing each piece individually.

From personal experience, I know one of the biggest disservices I can do for most clients is to do only one session with them. From what I have witnessed with clients in the past, they have this one session, create big goals and the start of a plan on how to get there, then spend the next six months with distractions and side routes before they call me back. It is much more effective to have at least four sessions where we can create the goals, lay out a real game plan for attaining them, begin holding them accountable for the steps, and do adjustments along the way. Their chance of success goes up exponentially by having the additional sessions. So I price my sessions by making it more affordable as the number of sessions goes up and to actually discourage the purchase of just one session.

"People don't care how much you know until they know how much you care." --John C. Maxwell

Promotion:

The final P is promotion. How are you going to promote what it is that you are offering?

Here I will encourage you to go back to the "Getting Nichey" chapter and really determine who your ideal client is. If you absolutely know who your ideal client is, promotion becomes that much easier because now you understand who they are and how to get what you offer in front of them. You understand what their problems truly are and how you solve them. You can discover their vocabulary and use that in your promotion: 30-second commercial, website, business cards, brochures, etc. You can determine the best avenues to use to have them actually find your information.

Public speaking / sharing your passion:
The fastest and best way I know to build a Lightpreneur™ business is to get out and speak about it. Forget about public speaking; share your passion about what you do. If you think of it as public speaking, then all of the fear that many people have associated with public speaking can come up. When I think of public speaking, I think of the mundane. Share your passion with groups of people. If you can help one person experience a better life, is it worth it? When you think of it that way, it changes everything. Where do you share your passion? Everywhere! Start out with community groups, civic organizations, women's / men's groups, church groups, community centers, shops that are in alignment with what you do, libraries, and, if all else fails, your living room. The key is to get out there and get started. Remember "Ready, fire, aim"? The more you are out there, the more opportunities will present themselves.

Business cards:

If you do not have business cards, you are not in business. With digital printing, it is too easy and inexpensive not to have business cards. Remember the rules we have shared in the book: keep it simple, focus on the client, speak to their emotion, and again, ready, fire, aim! Your cards will change as your business grows, so just consider it part of your businesses evolution.

Websites:

Websites are much more important in this day and age than a fancy brochure, **especially** early on, since your business is going to be evolving quickly. A website can reflect changes almost instantly, while changing brochures takes time and money, not to mention all the ones that are already out there. Do not worry about having a lot of fancy flash presentations on your website. Fancy and complicated just drives your visitors away. Simple and to the point will serve you and your clients much better. You can always add pages and features later, even if it is just one page with basic information. Get something up. This brings me to another point, your email address. Does readingsbygreta@gmail.com sound like someone who is serious about business? Info@readingsbygreta.com sounds so much more professional or greta@readingsbygreta.com. This is extremely simple and inexpensive to accomplish, $10 or less per year. When you reserve your URL through most companies, they include email redirects for free. Then you can have the emails to your new email address go right into your gmail or hotmail or any other email account. You should get at least one simple page up as quickly as possible because most people know to use the last part of that email address as your website.

If you do not know what company to purchase a website address / URL through, we have suggestions on the http://www.Lightpreneurs.com website. Just go to the "Elmas Recommends" page, and you will see who we are currently recommending.

Social Media:
Another key area of promotion that is especially hot right now is social media. Social media has taken on a life of its own in a very short amount of time. There are a lot of people teaching how to use social media who, I believe, are just wrong on many levels. They are basically encouraging you to SPAM potential clients using these sites. The keyword in social media is "social". That should be your approach, to be social. Build relationships with people. They might not be your actual ideal client, but they may know and lead you to your ideal client. Think of when people come up to you and just start pitching their business. How does that make you feel? The same applies to social media. Create relationships. Be genuinely interested in people. Offer value in your communications. We will speak about two websites specifically: Facebook.com and Meetup.com. There are many other social media sites, and there are new ones every day. Focusing on these two does not necessarily mean they will be the best or work the best for you, however, they are the two that cover the greatest number of Lightpreneur™ businesses at this time. Look at who your ideal client is and where they are most likely going to spend their time on social media sites.

Facebook: In March of 2010, Facebook surpassed Google as the highest traffic website. It has over 500 million members. This is not a Facebook training session, but rather some ideas to get you started.

I hear so many reasons why people do not use Facebook, and I would like to address a few of those right off. The first excuse is that it will take too much time. If you are taking more than 30 – 45 minutes per day, on Facebook it is probably not so much for your business, but rather personal enjoyment (or addiction). As of the writing of this book, I already have thousands of friends and hundreds of fans by using, on average, just 30 minutes per day--15 minutes in the morning and 15 minutes in the evening. Even if you were putting in hours per day, would it be worth it if it helped grow your business? Most Lightpreneurs™ starting out have more time than money to create their business.

Another excuse I hear is that people will know too much about me and be able to get my personal data. This is simple: do not put information you do not want people to know on social media sites. You have control. You can actually "unfriend" people on Facebook and most other sites if you do not like their interaction with you.

Finally, "I do not know how to do it." Do we even need to say "Ready, fire, aim"? Just get started. Find someone who already knows how and have them coach you through it. Take a class. Or just play with it and be OK with making a few mistakes along the way.

Most people who start using Facebook are amazed at the connections they make. My sister, who is one of the most "non-computer" people I know, thoroughly enjoys Facebook. She has been shocked at the connections she has remade through this website, including old school friends, childhood friends from her original hometown, and distant family she had lost contact with. So how do you use it to create awareness for your business? Simply put, by leaving breadcrumbs. Instead of spamming people or blatantly advertising, be yourself and put appropriate, valuable information that impacts people's lives. On your personal page, talk about yourself. This does not have to be anything too personal that you do not want to reveal. Give people a taste of who you are as a person and a look inside your character. People do business with people they like. On your fan page, give people a glimpse at the character of your business. You can do this through a variety of postings including quotes, your personal observations based on what your business is, or resources that help people you are trying to reach.

How do you work Facebook in 30 minutes per day? Split the time up into two parts: 15 minutes in the morning and 15 minutes in the evening. The first thing I do is post a personal update. This can be what my outlook is for the day, a class I am excited about teaching that day, or a video or article link others might enjoy. As for the class I am teaching, this is one of my best business builders. It is very non-threatening to people because I am obviously not trying to sell them because it is too late. What it does is open their curiosity so they ask me questions about when I might offer it again, etc. This exchange is out there for the world to see. The next thing is to post on your fan page something along the lines that we mentioned earlier. These are actually not the most important posts. Your most important posts are comments to other people's posts. That way you are being exposed to their friends list. This expands the awareness of you and what you do beyond your own friends list and draws more people to be your friends and fans.

Finally, go to the "people you may know" and click on "see all." You can right click on a person's name or picture and use "open in new tab." Get a feel for who they are. Click on "Add as friend" and send a personal message. I have a basic message that I cut and paste to insert in the message area. It talks about how they might look familiar and that they were in Facebook's "people you may know," and based on our mutual friends, it seems we are in many of the same circles. Type in their name and then paste your message with any changes and send it. Working your friends list for a few minutes a day is one of the fastest ways to initially build your friend list. Once you have a number of people as friends, you can invite them to "fan" or "like" your business page and grow that list very quickly.

There is another powerful aspect of Facebook: ads. Do not let this scare you away. *Facebook ads* are simple and inexpensive. If you use their pay-per-click program, you only pay when someone clicks on your ad. The beauty of this is that you can target your ideal client. You can specify where the people who see your ad live, their age and education, along with many other aspects, and then use keywords to narrow it down to people who would most likely have an interest in what you have to offer. We will not go into too much detail here because the information does change fairly regularly. If you would like more information on this and other current methods of promotion, make sure to check the Lightpreneurs.com website and sign up for the Lightpreneurs™ newsletter for the most up-to-date resources and information. For one Facebook ad campaign, we had 186 clicks and over 350,000 impressions, or people seeing the ad, for only $76. I have done a lot of advertising, and that type of return is unheard of with other media. As you see, the entire book could be on social media and Facebook specifically, so we will leave the rest for a different book or class. Also the information that will create the greatest benefit changes too quickly to do justice in a book. By the time the book is produced and released, there is new information that might be more impactful. I would suggest looking for one of our classes, webinars, or teleseminars on this subject and even newer methods of promotion for the most up-to-date information.

Meetup: Another powerful website you can use is meetup.com.   This website allows people to create interest groups and then post events to that group. You can go to the site and search the categories and groups to see any that are of interest to you and what events they have coming up. If you are looking for places to share your passion, this is a great place to start. Not all groups will be open to you coming in to speak for them because they are marketing their own products and services, but many are always looking for new speakers and activities. Send messages to as many appropriate groups as possible. Even if most are not interested in having you come in to share what you do, it only takes a couple to get you started building your business and making connections.

The most powerful way to use Meetup is by becoming an organizer.   There is a small fee involved to be an organizer, but if you search the internet, you can usually find coupons to reduce that cost even more. Becoming an organizer allows you to set up three different groups under the same organizer account. This will allow you to set up groups that give you a venue to share your passion as we discussed earlier. When you establish a new Meetup group, the most important aspects are the keywords. Shortly after you set up your group or when you schedule your first Meetup, meetup.com will email an announcement about your new group to everyone who has your keywords in their category interest list in that geographic area. If you set up your keywords correctly, you will be amazed at the number of people who join your group immediately. You can use Meetup for free presentations and even some of your paid events. These are just the simplest ways to use Meetup. There are many strategies that you can use with Meetup that is beyond the scope of this book, but just get started with it and grow as you go.

To finish off our discussion, we will briefly mention a few other social media sites. If you are working the corporate world, Linkedin is one of the big players there. This has become the de facto "social" media connector for big business with people seeking jobs, landing accounts, and building business networks. For the art community and much of the younger generation, MySpace is a perennial favorite. Ning.com is a way to create your own social media site. Ning is in flux at the writing of this book, so we are not sure how or what it is going to look like by the time you are reading this.

To conclude this chapter, we will reiterate the importance of the ideal client and getting to know them better than you know yourself. This way you can create awareness so they can understand what you are offering and how it will benefit them and offer them the end result that they are looking for. That is what you want to convey to that ideal client in an efficient, cost effective manner. You will better understand exactly what services and products to offer them and how to package them to make it have the greatest impact. You can create pricing and "package" strategies to offer the best value to the client while honoring yourself and your products / services. By focusing your marketing efforts on your ideal client, you can express how much you care about THEM.

Chapter 11

The Pareto Principle
A Powerful Force in Your Life

One of the basic laws of the universe is gravity. Another one that many of you are familiar with is the Law of Attraction. But there is another law that affects you personally. It affects your business and your success, and that is the Pareto Principle, which is also known as the 80/20 rule. The Pareto Principle is named after Italian economist Vilfredo Pareto, who, back in the early 1900s, observed that eighty percent of the land in his native Italy was owned by just twenty percent of the population. He then looked at his garden and realized that twenty percent of the pea pods in his garden accounted for eighty percent of the actual peas that it produced. Two entirely different circumstances had almost the exact same mathematical equivalent. Let me explain this in more modern day terms with something that probably affects you a lot more.

I guarantee you, if you go to a grocery store, approximately twenty percent of the items on the-shelves account for over eighty percent of all their total sales. Think about it. Bread, milk, meats, and the basics are strategically placed around the perimeter and rear of the store so you have to walk all the way through the store or to the back in order to get the basic things you need. This draws you across the other eighty percent of the items in the store. Grocery stores try to create additional sales from the other eighty percent of items that would normally only account for twenty percent of their sales. In the area of sales with companies that employ over 20 sales people, generally twenty percent of the sales force account for eighty percent or more of the sales. This is the general rule of thumb, but it does not vary much. Sometimes it is 70/30. More often than not, it tends toward ninety percent accounting for ten percent. If eighty percent of a resource is creating twenty percent of the benefit, then conversely twenty percent of any resource will account for eighty percent of the benefit.

How does this affect you and your business? Eighty percent of what you do in your life, eighty percent of what you do in your business, does not create a significant impact on your life, on your personal life, on your family, on your friends, on your business, or on your clients. Eighty percent of what you do could be left undone, with very little impact on your life. Let me take this out a little further so you can see how to use this to your advantage and create benefit in your life, the lives of the people around you, and the lives of your clients and prospective clients.

The first area I want to touch on is that twenty percent of the prospects you talk to are your actual clients. Let me say that again. Twenty percent of people you talk to are your real or, as I call them, your ideal clients. Eighty percent of the people you talk to are not your clients. For whatever reason, they do not want your service, they do not need your service, and you cannot convince them that they need your service. Eighty percent of the people out there will not listen to you. If you do a presentation to 20 people, only four of those are actually your ideal clients. Sixteen of those will not buy your product, or if they do, they are going to drive you crazy wanting more of your time or wanting something fixed or some other drain on you that keeps you from creating real benefit for others.

Here's how dangerous this is: I see so many Lightpreneurs™ do a presentation where there is a room of 20 people and 16 of them are not getting it or do not want anything else, and they start to leave. So the Lightpreneur™ focuses their energy on chasing after those people, trying to convince them that if they understood all the facts, they would jump on what is offered, and they follow them out of the room, trying to convince them of the benefits. I referred to the quote by Brian Tracy, "A man convinced against his will is of the same opinion still," in the "Getting Nichey" chapter. We can spend a lot of time, energy, and resources trying to convince those people, while back in the room, four people are waiting. They want to know what the next step is. They are hungry to take this to the next level, but you are putting all of your energy, all of your attention, or at least eighty percent of it, on the people who do not care and who are not going to embrace what you are doing instead of focusing that energy on the people who really will get the biggest benefit from what you have to offer.

This first aspect we are talking about with the Pareto Principle can change the way you do your business. It can change the amount of energy you exert to get the same number of clients or more. Instead of focusing on the eighty percent, focus on the twenty percent. Do the presentation and focus on those four. Turn them into clients. Create the benefit for them. If you want 20 clients, instead of doing a presentation to 20 people and trying to convince all of them that they are your clients, do a presentation to 20 people 5 times, and then you will get your 20 clients. You will actually spend a lot less energy, and they are going to be better customers for you because they will be your real customers, your ideal clients. By focusing on them, you are going to create what I call "missionaries." These missionaries are going to go and help you tell other people about you and the benefits that you offer, and they will help you find people just like them, more twenty percent people, and bring them to you instead of you having to exert the energy to go out and get them.

The second way the Pareto Principle can help you in your business is by understanding that twenty percent of the clients you have at any given time will account for eighty percent of your business. If you really look at this, it is a powerful concept. By creating feedback and follow-up systems in your business, you can identify who those twenty percent are so you can service them even better, they continue with you, and they tell even more people about you. Also identify what makes those clients your twenty percenters. What are their characteristics? What is their demographic? What is it they are looking for that makes them your ideal client? What is it that is missing from their lives that makes them account for eighty percent of your business?

If you already have a practice, look at your client base right now. I can guarantee you that you have certain clients who will always buy sessions from you, who are buying products from you, who are buying everything you offer and greater quantities of it than the average client does. The other eighty percent are only buying one or two things. They are getting a little bit of impact from you. You know they could get a lot more, but they are not committing to do it. They are the eighty percent. Focus on those twenty percent. Identify what makes those clients the twenty percent, and go out and find more clients exactly like them. Now that you know who they are, you can create your marketing pieces around this so there is a common voice that speaks directly to them in their vocabulary.

The third aspect that I want to share with you about the 80/20 rule is that twenty percent of what you offer will account for eighty percent of your business or impact. You may only offer one product or one service, but twenty percent of what you do in that service, and your products, are what draws eighty percent of your business to you. If you have multiple products or services, I know that you can identify which bring the lion's share of your business. If you have four things, I know that you can identify one of those things that accounts for the majority of your business.

With this knowledge, you, your business, and the impact you can create will be even more powerful! Now I want you to identify first what those twenty percent products or services are, and next ask yourself, "Why are they your twenty percent products?" What about them makes your clients buy them more? What about them creates the biggest impact for your clients? What about them is the thing that is really holding your business together? Once you can identify that, offer more products and services that have that twenty percent quality to them. Start shedding some of the eighty percent and focus more of your resources, more of your time, more of your dollars, more of your energy into the twenty percent aspects. But also identify what makes those the twenty percent so you can create new products, new services, that have those same qualities, so that your clients are going to want to use these also, and they are going to magnify your business and magnify the light that you put into the world.

The final aspect that I am going to talk about in relation to the Pareto Principle is probably the one that can create the greatest impact on your life in the least amount of time. This can be a little tough for people to really embrace because it completely goes against how they have been living their lives. But if you are honest with yourself and with how your day goes, you will realize how much this is directly impacting your life. If you take a hard look at your life, what you are doing each and every day is also being influenced by the 80/20 rule. This is to say that twenty percent of the items on your "to-do" list account for eighty percent of the benefit. The scary thing about this is that as you really look at it, eighty percent of the things on your "to-do" list do not matter. They do not create any real difference in your life, in your family's life, in the people around you, in your finances, your business, or for your clients. Where do we tend to spend most of our time? We spend the greatest portion of our time on the eighty percent things that account for only twenty percent of the impact. We waste away our lives on things that if we are honest with ourselves, would not matter if we did not get them done.

Look at your "to-do" list. What would happen if fifty percent of the things on it actually never got done? And I know some of you are stressing out just over the thought of them not getting done. But I want you to consider the things that create real impact in your life that you are **not** getting done because you are spinning your wheels doing all those things that do not matter.

I love going over people's "to-do" lists with them. It is so interesting to watch when they shift all their stuff that did not get done today over to the next day. You look at it, and three months later, they still have things that were on their "to-do" list months ago that they keep meaning to get around to, but never quite get done. It's all just a distraction. When they do get some of those things done, it really does not matter if they were done at all. Otherwise they would have been done three months ago. The real impact is that we load all of these things that do not matter on our "to-do" list, and it distracts us from the important things getting done. We keep putting them off. We procrastinate and avoid them because of fear or avoidance or whatever it is. But we keep ourselves really busy. We feel busy, then tired, then frustrated, and finally guilty when the important things still need to be done. We justify, blame, and/or ignore all the time that we are losing out on things that would be creating an amazing life for us.

Have you ever done a task and then gone and written it on your "to-do" list so just so could mark it off. Did that really mean anything? No! So I want you to forget about the "to-do" list. I want you to create a "could-do" list. If you will take just 5 minutes to do this, what you do is take those things that may have been on there for months and you have not gotten to and put those on your "could-do" list. Take an honest look at it. Start by marking off the things that are not going to be the end of the world if they do not get done today. By not doing them today, you are going to have more time and energy for the twenty percent that count. Do not start out by trying to slash all of the eighty percents. It will be too overwhelming. To start, I would like you to remove only twenty percent of your list and leave eighty percent on there. That helps you to start getting the idea and the feel of it. Allow yourself to start getting the concept and creating the change without causing overwhelming fear.

Now you are going to create a "possibility" list. Look at the eighty percent of things that are left once you knocked off the twenty percent, that you know really do not create a lot of impact, but are taking a lot of your time and energy, and create your "possibility" list. Start working from that. After you have done this for a few days, I want you to take that "could-do" list and knock out 50 percent of the things on there. Now you are starting to understand that you did not get them done and the world did not come to an end, but you had more time to do the things that were important. It is actually going to add to your life because you are using your resources much more efficiently. You're going to take the items off your "could-do" list and move them over to your possibility list.

Once you get really good at this, I want you to move beyond the possibility list. You are going to go from your "could-do" list, which is your old "to-do" list, to your "impact list," and this is the list that you take and just dive right into it, just like jumping into a pool. You are going to dive in head first to these things because these are the things that are going to create an impact in your life, in your family's life, in your business, for your clients, and for the world. Your "impact list" contains the twenty percent items that will create massive results and impact. Once you get the items on your "impact list" done, you could always go back to your "could-do" list and take a few of the things and do those, but only after you have created the real impact in your life.

Out of all of the material in this book, of which I've been presenting different aspects of for several years, this single area, applying the Pareto Principle to the old "to-do" list, will create the biggest difference in your life. This one thing will create such a big difference in your life that it will be hard to understand how you ever did it the old way and accomplished anything.

Your job now is to start identifying the twenty percent items in every aspect of your life and business. The first one was identifying the twenty percent of the people you are talking to and what makes them the people who become your clients. The second task is once they are a client, identify which of those are your twenty percent clients so you can see who you can create the biggest impact for with the least amount of resources. Continue to look at the products and services you offer, refine them, and create the greatest impact you can by looking at the twenty percent. Finally, get rid of your "to-do" list. Come up with the "could-do" list, then move that into your "impact list" and remember, you can always come back and pull a few items off of your "could-do" list once you create the real impact in your life. Knowledge is power. Now you have the additional knowledge of one of the laws of the universe. You may not have realized this law was influencing your life and your business. Now that you have the knowledge, I want you to go out and use that power to create the greatest impact for your business, your clients, and yourself.

Chapter 12

Opening Doors
To Your Success
Products and Services

Working with Lightpreneurs™, probably the biggest challenge I see facing them is that most of them are trading time for money. They generate cash flow by doing a "session" for a client using their time and talents, and the client gives them money in exchange. So for a practitioner in this situation, there are really only two ways to generate more cash flow to cover business or personal expenses. The first one of these is to work more hours. There are several problems associated with working more hours. The first issue is that when the practitioner is working more hours, they just get tired and start running out of the reserves they need in order to give the client what they really should be receiving. The practitioner feels like they are cheating the client and like they are being cheated themselves because they are so worn out that it just is not working anymore. So it becomes a catch-22 that just keeps circling around and around. The other aspect of this is the fact that once a practitioner does start working more hours and has more client sessions, they will get to the point where they are not marketing enough, so the number of client sessions will start to decline. In order to raise the number of client sessions back up, they need to get back out into the community and spend time marketing what they offer to get the number of sessions up. They are still working very hard, but their income goes down because they have to shift time away from working with clients, trading time for money, to gaining new clients or bringing old clients back into the fold. I have witnessed many successful Lightpreneurs™ get caught up in this trap, and after a few years, they just get so tired of it that they quit because they cannot generate enough cash flow in order to sustain their lifestyle and business.

Opening Doors To Success!

Session
$100

Is the price of entry presenting a barrier to potential clients entering your business?

The other way to generate more cash flow when you are trading time for money is to raise your fees. This has a diminishing return affect. The more you raise your fees, the less the clients are willing to pay them. Your income starts to stagnate even though you are charging more, and it actually begins to fall off after a certain point. Some practitioners struggle with valuing themselves or their services enough to do this, or they just do not feel integrity by continuing to raise the prices on their clients just so that they can make more money.

Look at the illustration and imagine that your business, and specifically the service you offer, is a doorway. Let's say the entry fee for that doorway is $100. Some of you may be charging more, some of you may be charging less, but I think you will get the point either way. If someone does not know you and the benefit they might receive, you can tell them all day long how great it is going to be, how amazing your modality is, but if they have not received it in any way, I can guarantee you there are a lot of people who cannot or will not pay that $100 entry fee to get through that doorway. So now, you essentially closed the door on a large number of your clients who are not willing to put in the proper key in the form of money to open that door.

At this point, I am going to encourage you to open a second door. I am going to highly recommend for this door, that the entry fee be *free* or complimentary. It could be a one-hour free presentation. I think we can all agree that a lot more people will be willing to go through the door where the entry is free than the one where there is a $100 fee. This way, they come in this door and get a taste of you and what you have to offer.

Here is the best way I know how to formulate this free presentation. If you have an hour to present, then you give them 45 minutes of raw, unfiltered information. They should feel like they are being washed over with information during those 45 minutes. Use the first fifteen minutes to get to know the crowd and let them get to

Opening Another Door

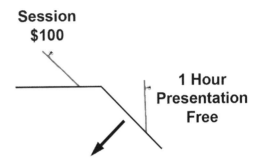

Session
$100

1 Hour
Presentation
Free

Opening an additional door will start to remove the barrier for some of your potential clients.

know you and build that rapport and some level of comfort with the group at the beginning of your presentation. The last five minutes, if you have flowed information over them and you are the source of information on this, not only do you have permission, but they will expect you to share how they can receive more of what you have to offer. Here's the other amazing thing about this. If you are the one who educates them about the benefits of hypnotherapy, energy work, life coaching, yoga, or any new concept, you have put yourself in the position of being the expert, and you are the one they will feel comfortable with. So when they are ready to partake in this and pay the entry fee, you are the one they will turn to because they already feel comfortable with you and know that you have the knowledge. They already have a connection with you. This is one of the fastest ways I know to build a business.

I want to pause a second here from talking about the doors and talk about that most feared thing to all humans: public speaking. I want to tell you here to just *get over it*. What I am asking you to do is not to go out and do public speaking, because public speaking is normally about a dry subject or something you are not passionate about. What I want you to do is share your passion. If you are not passionate about what you do in your business and the benefits you have to offer, then I would ask you to actually readdress what your business is. If you are in this as a Lightpreneur™, you should be passionate about it, and people will feel that passion. So when you get in front of an audience, I do not want you to worry about the audience at all. I want you to go into it with the intention of sharing your passion. If there is just one person out there whose life you can make a difference in, if there is one person out there who needed to hear what you had to say, isn't it all worth it? That is where your focus should be. If you keep your focus there, then it becomes so much easier and worthwhile.

The biggest key I can offer you to building your business is to get out and share what you are passionate about so that people feel your passion. Now they will have an understanding for what you do and be more willing to partake in your services.

Another interesting thing about getting out and speaking is that the money is not the only barrier to a new potential client doing a one-on-one session with you. For most people, the thought of sitting down face to face with someone they do not know, who does something they do not know much about, is very frightening. They may feel that they do not know you well enough or trust you enough to possibly share their deep, dark secrets with you. No matter if it is money, health, relationships or almost anything else you can think of offering, they will probably feel vulnerable sitting down with a "stranger." By sharing your passion and building that trust from the front of the room, you can go from stranger to someone they feel they can trust. Many times it is not about the money, but rather, fear of judgment. Help them remove the barrier of fear so they can receive the benefit you have to offer.

Opening Doors To Success!

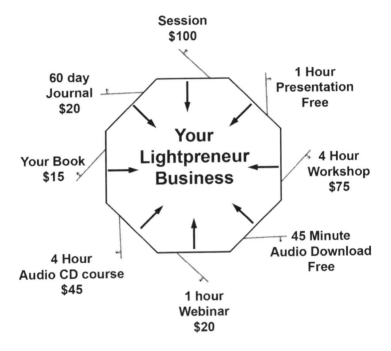

Do not get overwhelmed with the thought that you should have all of these before you start. Create a couple and then just keep adding. These are just a few ideas. There are so many more: teleseminars and webinars, workbooks, retreats, member programs, etc.

In regard to additional doors, I invite you not to have just a free session to educate them more, but I want you to have more educational opportunities for them. Open a third door which might be a four-hour presentation. This four-hour presentation is taking the information they started to receive to a deeper level and giving them some experiential learning around it. Now I ask you, do you think there are people who will come through a door and pay $75 for four hours, but will not pay $100 for your one-on-one hour? Of course there are. There are some people who will and some who will not, but I think there is a greater majority who will, especially if they have experienced you through the one-hour free presentation. Their perception is that they are getting a much better deal by doing this than paying $100 for a one hour session. Some people will never do a one-on-one session with you because they are going to try to take your information and do it on their own. They may start down that road and then get to the point where they want to go to the next level, and now they really want to work with you one-on-one. There is no way they would have ever gotten to that point, even with the best advertising in the world, without being able to see what you had to offer first and put it into practice on their own. But now, they want more.

Now, open a fourth door. Perhaps a 45-minute audio download. Where does this come from? You create it from the content portion of your one-hour free presentation. This will benefit people who are not close to you geographically or who do not have the time to go and listen to a one-hour presentation that you are giving at a specific time, in a specific place. This allows them to download it and listen to it at their leisure. Audio recordings are the fastest growing segment of the publishing arena right now because more and more people are listening to them while they are in their car or at the gym or hiking up a mountain. This allows them the freedom to experience the presentation, at least the spoken part of it, no matter where they are at. Once again they get a taste of you, what you do, and your passion around it, and there are a lot of people who will come through this door that would not be able or willing to come through any of the other three doors. So I think you are starting to get the idea here. We are opening new doors of opportunity for your clients to get to you and removing as many potential barriers as we can.

The next door I am inviting you to open is a four-hour audio recording. Once again, you get this from your four-hour presentation. This makes your work so much easier and creates more impact by doing work once and letting it benefit you and your clients many times over. You can even allow them to purchase it on your website as a download; just offer it cheaper since you do not have to ship it or manufacture it. Or you could offer it as a four-CD set that you could sell at your one-hour free presentation or to someone who is your one-on-one client.

This is a little precursor to what is about to happen with all of these doors. You know the question I am about to ask. Are there people who would buy a four-hour CD at $45 who might not come to your four-hour workshop because they do not have the time or are not close to you geographically? Are there people who do not understand your passion about what you do and the benefit that they would gain by paying to come through your regular session door? You know that the answer is yes. There are many people who will experience a deeper understanding of what you do and how it will benefit them and really embrace it, even though they would not have come through any of the other doors first.

Now I am going to go through a couple of other examples of doors you might be opening. One might be a teleconference series. Imagine doing four one-hour teleconference sessions, where you can sit at home and, using a conference call service, people dial in and participate in your four-hour presentation over a matter of four weeks instead of having to show up somewhere for four hours all in one sitting. They can just call in on the phone while the kids are in the other room, while they are just taking a break from work, whenever and wherever they can fit this in. Once again, do you think there are people who would pay $65 for a 4-hour teleconference but would not pay for the one-on-one session? Another example is webinars. This is where you use an online service to make a presentation. They can hear your voice, and if you have a PowerPoint presentation or a movie presentation, you can include that also. This just magnifies the impact you can create and takes away the geographical limitations. Then anyone in the country or in the world can participate in what you are doing. There are many free services for webinars and teleseminars. If you need help finding these or other resources for your Lightpreneur™ business, go to www.lightpreneurs.com and click on "Elmas Recommends" from the drop down menu.

Another door you can open is writing a book. I know that if you are a Lightpreneur™, you have a book in you, whether you believe it or not. Having written this book, with several more on the way, I can tell you that writing a book does not have to be difficult, especially for a Lightpreneur™. You should be able to easily write a book about what you do and what you are passionate about. The book you are reading was created from the information that was already being used in a "Calling All Lightpreneurs™" presentation. Remember what we mentioned earlier about doing work once and letting it create benefit over and over. We actually recorded the information and had it transcribed. The book practically wrote itself. Of course there was editing to be done to go from spoken to written word, but the "hard" part of sitting down and doing the writing was done.

A book is another door that more and more people would be willing to enter without going to your presentation or experiencing you in any other way. You get to share a piece of who you are through that book, and with this, they start to get to know you and believe in what you are offering. Self-publishing is becoming so much easier. Instead of making less than a dollar for the books you sell, you can be making the majority of the profit. You can easily be making $10 to $15 per book.

As we are finishing the "Calling All Lightpreneurs™" book, we are creating a new program called Passion To Published™. It is designed specifically to help Lightpreneurs™ write their book with the end goal of creating the greatest impact for their clients. We use methods that make writing that book easy and fun. Even if you have tried to write your book in the past and not succeeded or just don't know how to start, trust me, you can do it. If you would like more information on this program, go to www.passiontopublished.com. As with having a business, my philosophy is that writing should be fun and easy. If it is not, fire yourself and start over.

Our last potential door we are going to be talking about is a journal. Journals can be amazing tools for your clients and can be very easy for you to write and produce. Many of your clients are already journalers. People journal or keep diaries for many different reasons. For Lightpreneurs™, this can become a powerful asset for a large number of your potential clients. Imagine your clients being guided to do some inner reflection around whatever it is you are helping them with. Every day for 30, 60, or 90 days they have a different thought or question to ponder and journal around. This gives your clients an amazing, powerful tool to further them in their journey. It usually creates information and insights to help you, as the Lightpreneur™, to move the client along even further and faster. It magnifies what you do and can be used with other aspects of your business. This can be used, along with any of the other doors, to create packages of services to give your clients greater value and benefit with less of your own personal resources. To create a journal, you just need to come up with 30, 60, 90, or 365, depending on how long you want it to be, journal questions or thoughts. You expand these by adding lines and blank areas. To start out, you could possibly print them out yourself and have a local print shop bind them with a cover. This normally will cost you a couple of dollars for something you can easily sell for $20. It is NOT the paper, the ink, and the cover they are buying. That is just the vehicle that carries what they truly want, the information. They are spending their money for the knowledge, the process, the change, and the benefit.

There is another door that is not on the illustration that we will mention, and that is workbooks. It is much like a journal in that it is easy to make, inexpensive to produce, and can create amazing benefit. They really help your clients take your message and put it into practice in their own lives. Take a workshop that you are doing and use your notes or PowerPoint as a guide. Go through the information and ask yourself what question you could ask someone to have them work through the information for themselves. Once you have created all of the questions, have someone read them over and tell you which areas need more information to take them back to the material in your presentation and bring them closer to implementing it. Put in lines or blank areas for them to answer the questions, and have it printed. Workbooks can be a powerful way to have clients do independent work. Think of how many people go to workshops or presentations or read a book, and then life gets in the way and two weeks later, they are not applying the tools or information. Workbooks give them something tangible as they put the tools and information into action and apply them to their own lives. I mentioned earlier that this book was based on information from a presentation I was doing. Now we are creating a companion workbook to go along with the information so readers can apply it to their own situation and put it into action rather than this just being another book that they read and have every intention of using but becomes forgotten in the shuffle of life.

You can create the workbook from your four-hour presentation or your teleconference. You can even do it as an e-book so they can download it from your website. This may sound like a lot of details, but remember what I said about not getting caught up in it. One of my big jokes is that if you do not know how to use technology, find a 12-year-old. All the kids today know how to do this stuff on a computer. I am being funny here, but at the same time, not. If you are hung up on the details, find someone who will not be and have them help you through this process.

I want to go back to something I already mentioned. Imagine you are doing a one-hour free presentation. People do not know who you are, but they are coming there and they get to experience you for free. Imagine that you have your book available for them. You will sell books if you do this! Imagine that you have your four-hour CD there also. You are going to sell CDs too. Maybe you have your book on audio. We had a home study course on teaching people how to create their own audio products very easily and extremely inexpensively. If you are doing small quantities, You can produce them on your own to get started and leverage your business. The software we were using changed, but we are planning on coming out with a new version in the very near future. Make sure you are signed up for our newsletter at www.Lightpreneurs.com website to see when that course is available if that is daunting task for you. It does not have to be, and it can be a huge component for your business.

I want you to look at this little house that we have created, this little, 8-sided house. Where do all of these doors lead? They lead directly to you. They lead directly to helping you generate the cash flow you need to keep doing what you need to be doing. They lead to more ways to create benefit for your current and potential clients. Some of the people who come to you are not really into going to a presentation, but they might be into reading a book. Some people do not have the time for either, and they might listen to the four-hour CD. You have people out there who love to journal, and you have the ones who just want the one-on-one session. So you open these extra doors to give them additional ways to receive the benefit of what you have to offer, and in return, they help generate more cash flow. So imagine this: somebody comes to your one-hour free presentation; they buy your book; they like the information there. They go to your four-hour presentation. Then they realize that they want to take it to the next level, and now they start paying your hourly fee to have one-on-one sessions with you. They have already received a greater benefit by the time they come to that session because they have the foundational pieces of your services, so now you can hit the ground running with them. You can create a better session because they are now ready to be in that moment with you, and they are fully engaged and ready to go.

Do not get overwhelmed with thinking that you have to open eight doors all at once for your business to get started. That is not the case. But I do want you to open three, four, or even five doors very quickly so you have additional ways to not only benefit your client, but to give them a taste of who you are so they are more likely to come in and receive the full benefit of what you have to offer. There are an unlimited number of doors, and we have only mentioned a few here. There are so many more possibilities such as: doing group work, a card deck, smart phone apps, retreats just to name a few. I have clients who have created games and interactive web experiences. That can all be down the road, but understand that once you create these doors, you are creating multiple income streams. I want you to remember the concept we discussed earlier that buyers are buyers are buyers. As you open new doors, previous "buyers" will buy again, creating additional benefit for them and additional income for you.

So take a moment, sit down, and, based on what your business is, what are 3 or 4 or 5 doors you can offer right now that will not take you long to create? The one-hour free presentation is just you sharing what you are passionate about, so that is an easy one to do. You already know what your one-on-one session is. Can you create a four-hour presentation, a workbook, or a journal? Which one would be easier for you? When you get right down to it, they all have very similar information, so you are not reinventing the wheel for every one of these doors; you are just offering a different vehicle that they can experience it through.

If you start looking at your business using this model, I think you can see how you can generate more cash flow to help you keep doing what you want to do and what you are supposed to do much more easily and faster than just trying to trade time for money. I also think you can see how to keep expanding your business. Think of some amazing examples of people who successfully offer their services in so many different ways. One of my favorites is Byron Katie, who created a wonderful process called "The Work." Then there are Esther and Jerry Hicks and their work with Abraham. They have multiple ways for people to experience their work, like books, CDs, webinars, live presentations, and even exotic trips. Wayne Dyer has his presentations, his books, his audios, and even presentations on television through PBS. Think of the big influencers out there right now, and I think you will see that they have many doors through which their potential clients may find and experience them.

So take a few moments. Discover what your baby steps are to start creating your first couple of extra doors. Once you get those doors and create a clientele, then look for a couple more and then a few more ways to expand on what you have to offer, and I think you will look back one day and see your business creating an amazing impact on the world.

Chapter 13

Systemize
For Success
Making Life Easier

In this chapter, we are going to be talking about creating systems for your practice. A lot of practitioners are resistant at first to thinking they can create systems for their practice because they never know what type of client they are getting next or what that client's problem is going to be. Practitioners do not always know exactly how they will start out with a new client.

Imagine working in an emergency room. I cannot think of any profession that is less predictable. You really never know what is going to come in the door next. It might be someone with a cold, or a person who was in a car accident, someone giving birth, or even someone having a heart attack. I believe you can agree this is an extreme example of not knowing what type of situation could walk through the door next. All hospitals have a system for their emergency room and every department therein.

Every single event that occurs in that hospital has a system. It is called protocol.

There is a protocol for what to do when someone walks through the door and for each person they encounter. Based on the situation, they are handed off to any number of other systems, depending on how critical the person is, the workload they already have, and the resources that are available. Each patient is moved through that system, whether it is diagnosis or treatment, and then they are passed on to another system, all the way through to releasing the patient either from the emergency room or from their stay in the hospital. So if a hospital which manages a wide array of diverse events can have systems for anything they may encounter, then surely you can start creating systems for your practice. I guarantee if you start doing this, it will make your life a lot easier, and it will make your future success a lot less daunting. We'll talk about how that works as we go through the chapter.

For our purposes, a system will be defined as a set of methods, procedures, or routines created and maintained, which, when performed, will benefit the whole. All we are saying here is that the more you create routines, the easier it will be for you to create the impact you are trying to create. This is especially true and beneficial for all of the real *business*-related tasks you do.

Take a look at the "Systemize for Success" illustration. You will notice that we have five "cogs": marketing, intake, service/product delivery, feedback, and follow-up. These are the most basic cogs for your business. You can break these down further to have cogs inside of cogs or sub-systems, but these are the most fundamental areas you should look at to create your business systems.

Systemize For Sucess

For many Lightpreneurs™, every time they go out to market their business, they are reinventing the wheel or cog. It is like starting from scratch each and every time. What if you just determined what worked and what did not work? For example, you could start jotting down the steps you take to place an ad. Do you think this might make it a bit easier the next time you place an ad?

The first of the five cogs in the illustration is marketing. Many times, that is the one cog that practitioners want to forget about entirely. But without marketing and creating that awareness of what you do, your potential clients will not be able to benefit. They simply will not know you exist. You are not going to benefit because you are not going to have the number of clients coming to you that you need to sustain yourself and keep doing this business. The more you systemize your marketing, the easier it will become over time. What am I referring to when I say to "systemize" your marketing? I want you to start writing down anything you do to create awareness of what you do and the services you offer. You may think that you do not have enough time to spend actually writing down the steps you are taking to place an ad, to create your marketing copy, or whatever it may be. But you do not have the time to waste *not* writing it down. Here is why I say that: if you write it down this time, then the next time you go through it, instead of having to remember what you had done in placing that ad in a periodical, lining up an event, or creating your marketing campaign, you just refer back to your notes. Now, you can easily move through the steps. It also helps you identify a step that you might have missed before or delete unnecessary steps. I cannot stress enough how important marketing is to your business. The sooner you get systems around this, the sooner you can identify what works and what does not.

The next focus in the 5-cog system is intake. It surprises me how many practitioners do not have any form of intake or at least a formal system of intake for a new client. When I refer to intake, I am talking about the moment someone says they want to be your client and an agreement is reached regarding what you will be doing for them and what they are paying. Whatever that may be, you need some way of processing them into the system. That sounds more cold and impersonal than it actually is. A good intake system will allow you to save time by cutting to the chase. In the intake, you can obtain information and start using it directly to create greater impact for your client. You can hit the ground running.

The intake goes from the simple details, such as their name, contact information, and how to follow-up with them later, to more specific information related to what you do in your practice. There may be questions about where they are right now, where they would like to be, how they would best like to be handled. I do this with all my clients. I have that system in place where the intake information is emailed to the client prior to meeting, and then they simply email it back. I can look this over prior to the client walking in the door or making the phone call, and now I am fully prepared and already have the process rolling. I already have the energy flowing and know where to start with this particular client. Those questions actually lead me to better questions once I am face to face or in direct contact with that client. My intake form is at such a level now, that my clients, before they even meet me, feel like they have gone through more coaching just by filling out the intake than they have done with other coaches after several sessions. They already feel as though they are in the coaching process, like they are already working on what they came there to work on. So they are already excited and ready to move forward.

That leads us to the next cog, which is the service you provide. Some of you offer more in the way of products, and that is fine, too. Make a system around both your services and products. They can be two entirely different cogs. In the service cog, start by focusing on the basics. This is where I get the most resistance from practitioners because this is where they think they cannot have a system. I guarantee you that there are some commonalities in the beginning part of how you work with any given client. So start debriefing yourself once you have concluded a session with a client and ask, "What were the commonalities?" How did I start this one? Is it similar to something I have already done in the past? You are going to recognize the common threads and what works. You have held them before unconsciously, and now you are going to be more conscious of what you are doing and how that really provides value for your client.

Some of you will be focusing more on products than on services. In creating your product cog, look at how you deliver it and how you produce it or have it produced, if done by someone else. Start systemizing all the different aspects of this, and I think you will see why this is so important. Ask yourself how you put it together. What did you print out? How did you record it? How did you do every single step? How did you package it for shipping? How did you ship it? If it is something you put on your website for a download, how did you load it on the website? The more you systemize this, the easier it is going to be to turn all those details over to somebody else so you can do the things that create additional impact for your clients. You can create additional products and services, or you can be out there in front of potential clients, sharing with them the benefits that these products offer.

The next cog is the feedback system. I encourage you to get feedback after an initial session, a presentation, and all the different aspects of delivery of your products and services. The reason this is so important is that your clients will tell you what new products and services they would like to see that would create amazing benefit in their lives. They will help you identify the most important doors, as we described in the "Opening Doors to Your Success" chapter. Also they can help you become more efficient in providing the most valuable aspect of your service. Remember when we talked about the Pareto Principle, the 80/20 rule? Twenty percent of what you do in a client's session accounts for eighty percent of the benefit they receive. A lot of times, as the practitioner, we lose sight of the true benefit our clients are receiving from our services. Our clients can tell us what aspect really launched them to the next level. Then we look at the delivery of the service or products we are offering and do more of *that* in our business. You can consider removing altogether the things that are not necessarily providing a benefit to the client. My clients who have really focused on this feedback aspect find they become so efficient at delivering their message that they create missionaries who go out and proselytize about them and the services they offer. These "missionaries" start generating more clients.

The final benefit of creating a feedback system is the fact that the feedback can go directly into your marketing in the form of a testimonial, or indirectly by discovering their vocabulary and the words your clients use instead of the buzz words *we* use in delivery of our service. By using their vocabulary, your potential clients will hear it in their own language and understand in their terms what you offer and the specific benefits they will receive. This feedback system can help make your marketing and intake systems more powerful because now you know more information to put in there that you did not know before. This one little cog seems so unimportant to so many practitioners, but it can become huge in making your business better, stronger, and have more impact on your clients.

I cannot emphasize enough the importance of testimonials. People love to hear about other people's experiences in their own words. Testimonials can be a gold mine for your business. One of the easiest ways to get testimonials is to write them yourself. Now I am not talking about doing anything unethical in creating fake testimonials. What I mean is, many people are afraid they are not going to do the testimonial right. They really want to give us a testimonial, but they are afraid it is not going to be what we want them to say. So an easy way for you to get a testimonial is to debrief your client or have someone do this for you by asking them specific questions. Then you can put their answers in a format and hand it back to them in a later session and ask them if they would mind you using this as a testimonial. Usually they are happy to do this.

I learned this when I was selling benefits packages in corporate America. I would have someone I was working with who would love to give me a testimonial, but they would get caught up in the business of their day and then they would be afraid that they were not giving me what I wanted, and they would have to do it again. I would usually ask them what they enjoyed about working with me and what they enjoyed about the services that I offered. Then I would come back a couple weeks later with some information typed up, which was essentially their answers to all those questions. Ninety-nine times out of 100, they would hand it to their assistant, have it put directly on their letterhead, and sign off on it. That made their lives easier and less stressful. So this is a big tip for you to use with your clients in getting those all-important testimonials.

Followup

The final system I am going to talk about here is your follow-up system. We spend so many resources--our time, our money, our energy--trying to attract new clients, when the most valuable new client we have is an old client we may have forgotten about, or more importantly, who has forgotten about us. Having a system for connecting with them and following up with them can become a whole new stream of income for your business that was just waiting to be tapped into. A lot of times our clients do not refer people to us because they do not know how. They do not know our 30-second commercial. They do not know our marketing emphasis. So if you give them some easy information, such as an email, they can easily share that with people. At first you want to follow-up by touching base with clients you may have forgotten; maybe life has gotten in the way and they have not scheduled an appointment or signed up for that next class with you. They have not purchased the next product you came out with because they forgot to, so you are just giving them a friendly reminder.

The second aspect of the follow-up is the educational piece of how they can refer more people to you. Have a system of how often you touch base with clients who have not been in--or even the ones who have been in--and educate them on how to refer people to you. If they like your service, then chances are they want to refer people to you. There is no better business than referral business. It is also a good area to come up with a process to reward clients for referring people. One of the things I like to do is give gift cards. I will actually ask somebody what restaurant they like to go to in their area. Then I will send them a gift card. For many practitioners, this has more integrity then giving cash for referrals. This is a gift you are giving to someone as a thank-you. What I want you to really look at is the average revenue from a client in your practice. What is their value? I would imagine for most of you, you do not do just one session. What is the average number of sessions you do with a client over the course of time that you work with them? What is the average number of classes? Some of them may be coming to classes and sessions, and so the average value of a client is going to be much more than one session. The average value of your clients is probably much more money than you realize. When someone brings a new client to you, even if your session cost is $75, the value of that referral is probably worth $300-$400, so it is easy for you to give a $25 or $50 dollar gift card. You are not losing anything at all. Now that person is going to remember you even more and will probably refer more clients to you. It is a definite win for you because you have a new client whose average value is going to more than cover the costs of the gift you have given to your client. The client is being rewarded, so they win from the gift you are giving them. The new client wins because they get to experience your services. Create as many win-win situations like this as you possibly can, and you will see your business grow exponentially, creating an additional win for you.

If you are still somewhat resistant to creating systems, let me give you the real secret as to why you want to create these systems. For many of you there is a fear of success; what if your business takes off and gets really big? You do not have enough hours in the day now to do what you are doing, and you do not even have that many clients. Let me just say if it gets that big, you do not have to go it alone. If you create these systems, it will be easy for you to turn over the marketing cog to someone else, and you can show them specifically how you have done things. You can even share with them the things to avoid, and now maybe they can even enhance your systems and bring in new ideas. They are not starting from scratch. They already have your systems, which are obviously working if you are getting enough clients to warrant bringing them on to take over the marketing aspect. This way your business will not take a hit when you turn it over to somebody. Your business will actually grow by them bringing more ideas to the table and not having to reinvent the wheel from the start. Also you can turn over the intake if you have an assistant coming in. They can make sure that the client gets the intake forms and that you get them back before your session. They can also look at those forms with a fresh set of eyes and make it an even better intake. So as you relinquish some of these aspects, it makes your job so much easier. As your business grows, instead of you being more inundated and having less energy, you will have more energy to directly interact with the client instead of covering all of the other administrative and marketing tasks as well. Because it is so easy to forget about the follow-up and the client we have not seen for the last several weeks, your assistant can take over and start generating more business than you ever thought possible.

For a select few of you that are reading this who have a system down for your service, it would be easy for you to train and have a certification program so you can leverage your impact even more by certifying people to do exactly what you are doing. By putting them under your umbrella if they agree to a code of conduct or a code of service, they continue doing some occasional, continuing education. This might free you up to do even more presentations, to generate more impact, to generate more people using your services or products. I think if you look around at some of the practitioners, the larger names you enjoy hearing about, you will find they have leveraged themselves in this way. Do not get overwhelmed with the thought of turning your business over to somebody else or even certifying other practitioners. I want you to take the baby step and start writing down your different systems. How you create awareness for your business. What forms do you use and what steps do you take for your intake? Systemize the delivery of your service and products and then systemize that feedback so you can start making your service and intake better and creating awareness for your company so much more easily. Finally, systemize that follow-up so that you can make sure nobody falls through the cracks.

Chapter 14

Creating Your
Vision to Success
Feel it, Believe It, See It

Imagine you have a puzzle laid out before you and all the pieces are jumbled up--a rather large puzzle with many, many pieces. You are about to try to put this intricate puzzle together, with all of its different colors and patterns. Then you realize you do not have the box that the puzzle came in. You do not have a picture, so you do not know what this puzzle is supposed to look like when it is completed. How difficult is it to put that puzzle together? You do not know what patterns or colors go together; you just have to start guessing at what might go where and how it all fits together. It is very difficult without knowing what that puzzle is supposed to look like when it is finished.

That is how most Lightpreneurs™ go about doing their business. They are trying to put a big puzzle together with all the details and all the systems, but they do not even know what the puzzle should look like when it is completed. They fumble around trying to figure out where the pieces are going and trying to force pieces together, and they get frustrated when the pieces do not seem to match up. Many people might even feel they have multiple puzzles all jumbled together because they do not know what the whole thing looks like. Knowing what your business is supposed to look like down the road will help you have a better idea of how to put those pieces together, figure out where all the pieces belong, and realize which ones actually do belong to your puzzle and which do not.

Now many people will encourage you to put together a business plan. For the sake of this book, I am *not* going to tell you that you must have a business plan, but I do want you to have a vision plan so that you know what the end result of your business is supposed to look like. You will know what all the pieces are and how they are supposed to fit together. A vision plan is much like a business plan, except it is more of a story format. Here I will lay out the basics, and if you understand these, then you can create a sufficient business plan to help drive yourself to success and create additional benefit for your prospective clients.

First, sit down and tell the story of different aspects of your business. The first part of the story you are going to tell would be called the story of awareness which is much like a marketing plan. Do not get hung up on the fact that it is a marketing plan, but rather, look at it as how you create awareness and what you are creating awareness of. If you were looking at a traditional business plan, you would be looking at the 4 P's: Product, Place, Price and Promotion. For Lightpreneurs™, in lieu of a product section, you will have primarily a service section, but as you already know from the "Opening Doors" chapter, I really want you to look at both products and services for your Lightpreneur™ business and how to create those additional doors. If you have not already started thinking about what doors you might open immediately, I want you to go back and look at that chapter and start brainstorming what doors you might open to create greater benefit for your clients and which ones create additional cash flow to support you and your Lightpreneur™ business. Begin the journey by telling the story about what products and services you offer now and what products and services you know you will be offering in the future to benefit your clients. Next, tell the story of where you will offer these products and services. Do you offer them directly to someone face to face, through the internet, over the phone? Are they offered through your website? Are you putting your book on

Amazon? Where are you going to place your products and services?

Now tell the story of how you are going to price these products and services. I want you to realize that this is a very key decision for your business. We already went through this in depth in the "Marco Polo" chapter, and pricing is so important that I encourage you to go back and review that chapter if you need a refresher course on it. You need to decide where your business falls on the price continuum, and as a Lightpreneur™, I encourage you to shy away from the low price end of the continuum. You can't have the volume of a Wal-Mart (a company that sells for a low price because of the volume they do) without affecting the quality, delivery, and customer aspects of what you do.

Am I suggesting that you be the highest price in the price continuum? Not at all. I have, however, seen more Lightpreneurs™ succeed on the higher end of the spectrum because, in so doing, they are able to give better quality customer service. They are able to offer hands-on help and continue doing what they are supposed to be doing for a much longer period of time.

A side note to this is to remember back to the chapter on "Abundant Gifts," where we talked about how the medicine person in the tribe was actually one of the wealthiest members of that community. You, as a Lightpreneur™, you, as a modern medicine person, should expect to have all of your needs met, and beyond. Be that example of prosperity for your clients.

The final consideration of your vision plan story is promotion. Now you really create awareness around all of the amazing benefits that you create. We already covered a little bit about that in other parts of the book, so

I am not going to dwell on it here. But I cannot emphasize enough the importance of creating that awareness of the true benefit you offer to your clients. You need to include this in the story of your business.

Once you have told the story of creating the awareness of your business, what the products and services are, where you are going to be offering these, what price you are going to be offering them at, and how you are actually letting prospective clients know about them, you need to move on to a different part of the story: how your business actually makes money. I want you to stop thinking of trading time for money. Create a story here of all the different ways that your company creates cash flow and the different ways that your money builds prosperity so you can continue doing what you love to do for a long time. Once again, look at all the doors and start showing how much each one of them brings in. Without getting into too much detail, project out into the future what you think you could be doing in three, six, and nine months, and also two to five years, so you can see the growth of your company and not just the products and services offered. Tell how it generates cash flow to support even bigger ventures, including expanding the product lines with higher end products to open even more doors. Tell the story of the operations of the company. Who are you? What makes you who you are as far as the benefit you offer to clients? Add a little of your background here. Do not get hung up on the details. Just tell the story. What is it about you that separates you and your business from everyone else? What makes you personally unique?

Now comes perhaps the most important piece of the entire business story process. You are going to read over your entire story and create a Reader's Digest version of that story. I want you to put this Reader's

Digest version on one page as a vision summary. If you are writing a business plan, this could be the same thing as the executive summary. It should not be more than a page. Many successful businesses, even large businesses, started out on the back of a napkin. If you cannot write the summary of your business, what it is, what products and services you offer, how you create awareness, and how you generate cash flow around it, on one page for someone else to understand, then your business is too loose. You need to tighten it up so that you can easily get the concept across. Once you get all this down, it would be quite easy to turn it into a formal business plan if you choose, but at least you have a vision plan now so you see what your business really is and where it's going tomorrow, the next day, and into the future. Now you can see where those puzzle pieces fit.

Lastly, I am going to encourage you to read your vision summary twice a day, every day that you work on your business. I want you to read it in the morning before you do anything with your business. This way it will set you up so that you know what your business really is, and it will remind you of both the important details and the details that are not important. Going back to the 80/20 rule, you can now identify the twenty percent items on your list of things to do. This will keep you motivated and moving along in the right direction, staying focused on what your business truly is. I also encourage you to read it at night before you go to bed so you can set the intention for the next day and know what you are supposed to be focusing on, but also so your subconscious mind, your higher source, can solve any hurdles or problems that are coming up. Do not read it in a state of worry. Read it in a state of expectancy; expecting solutions to come to you; expecting the next great idea to come to you; expecting to grow your business easily and with peace. If you take the time to write your business story or vision plan and then create the vision summary, I think you will be amazed at how focused you can become and how easily you can set aside the things that do not matter and really move your business forward to create prosperity for yourself and benefit for the world in ways you may not have been able to imagine before.

Chapter 15

Mirror, Mirror
On The Wall
What Is Your Business Reflecting?

Your Lightpreneur™ business is a reflection of yourself. We are taught that taking care of #1 is selfish, and many people look down on this. However, your Lightpreneur™ business is a direct reflection of how you are showing up in the world. If you are tired, it will show up in your business. If your personal relationships are strained, your business relationships will surely follow. If you are chaotic, your business will be also. I think you get the picture. Taking care of yourself is such an important piece

for Lightpreneurs™ that it could be a complete book in and of itself, and it will be a large part of an upcoming book, *The Complete Lightpreneur™*. Because of the significance self-care can have on the success of getting your Lightpreneur™ business started, we will highlight some of the most important concepts in this chapter.

When we talk about taking care of yourself, we are referring to all three aspects, including body, mind and soul or spirit. As a Lightpreneur™, you can be so busy helping others that you can forget to help or take care of yourself. This is a big mistake, and while it can seem like you are doing it to be of greater service to others, you are actually diminishing your level of service. There will less of you to give in both quantity and quality.

First off, you will burn out very quickly with this pattern of not taking care of yourself. Let's take for example, a horse. It gives service by taking the rider where it needs to go. But without adequate care, that horse is not able to take the rider the distance. Without proper food, water, rest, etc., the horse will give out long before its true capability has been met. Secondly, the more you go without taking care of yourself, the less you have to give your clients and your customers. If that horse is not shod properly or has an ill-fitting saddle, the ride will be rough, and the horse will be uncomfortable.

The biggest thing here is to check in with yourself on a regular basis to make sure that you are taking care of yourself in all three areas. I would suggest a minimum of once a week. It should be daily, but weekly is the absolute minimum. Pick a specific day of the week that you check in with yourself physically, mentally, and spiritually. Take an inventory of where you need to recharge your batteries and energize yourself so there can be more of you, as a Lightpreneur™, to give. Do this so you can keep doing your purpose for many years to come.

So what are some of the ways you should be taking care of yourself? First off, look at your practice or your business. Make sure that you are not "piling on" the clients or customers. Give yourself enough time between

166

appointments to relax, regroup, and re-energize. Your next client deserves it, and so do you. This holds for classes and presentations too. I have been guilty of this in the past myself by doing an all-day presentation and not taking breaks during the day. It is so easy to get sidetracked by "just a quick question" when you give the attendees a break, that the next thing you know, break is over and you never took one for yourself. If you are doing extended presentations, plan in sections where participants are doing the work, in pairs or groups, and use this opportunity to recharge and go to the restroom. Put a trusted person in charge of the room so you do not feel you must rush back.

Boundaries are another extremely important area. This is a deep, dark subject that many Lightpreneurs™ would rather not face. But you are hurting yourself and your clients if you do not set up specific boundaries for your practice. Boundaries are important for you and critical for your clients/customers. Without boundaries, you dis-empower your clients. Children do not function well without boundaries, and neither do adults. Good boundaries let people know where you end and they begin. You should have physical boundaries of where you meet clients. You and your client should be clear about where the boundary is. This allows both of you to feel comfortable and safe and removes stress. You should have time boundaries of when the "Open" sign is lit and when it is not. Being too available to clients disempowers them, and you become their crutch. If you are "always there for them," they do not have a chance to prove to themselves that they can start to do the work independently. There should be boundaries of exchange. You should not give without receiving. If your client is unsure of what that exchange actually is, it can create negative emotion, including: stress, anxiety, guilt, anger, frustration, etc. Depending on your practice, there are any number of additional boundaries you should consider setting.

Who is your client? We already discussed your "Ideal Client" in the "Getting Nichey" chapter, but it needs to be mentioned here. If your client drains you, how does that serve you or your purpose? If you stress over your clients, how long will you be able or want to continue? Your clients should energize you, not leave you drained. When I am living my purpose and creating a true impact on the world, it energizes me. I can work hard and feel a good tired that is not fatigue, but more like a physical workout that leaves me winded, but I know will just make me stronger. If your clients are leaving you exhausted and drained to the point where you have a hard time bouncing back, that is not making you stronger, but rather, making you and your work less and less effective. Part of this may be your attachment to the outcome. Always remember that it is the client's responsibility to change; it's not yours to change them. You can lead a horse to water... Give them the tools--empower them--but understand that what they do with that is their choice. I know that I want success for many of my clients even more than they want it for themselves. I cannot create it for them. That is not fair. It deprives them. It deprives them of their own power; of their own victory; of their own self-worth. Lead them by your words, your actions, and your teachings. Avoid the temptation to do it for them. You will last a lot longer and help more people in deeper ways by doing so. You will be the conduit for empowerment.

A lot of this comes down to having fun. You will hear me say over and over, if you are not having fun, fire yourself and start over. If you are not having fun in your business, why do it? If you are not enjoying it, how long will you last? If you are not planning on your business being fulfilling, why not just get a job? So create your business so that you enjoy what you are doing. Draw to yourself the ideal client who is ready, willing, and able to move forward. Create your business model to include the things that you enjoy doing.

Now let us look at the other key component of taking care of you, and that is YOU! What do you need physically to take care of yourself? Make sure you are eating properly, not just for fuel, but also for long term health. It is easy to get caught up and skip meals or eat things you know are not the best for you. Also, *move*. Whether it is exercise or just getting up out of the chair and walking around the block, move your body. It is amazing how stale our energy can be become when we remain stationary. Listen to your body and ask it what it needs. Pamper yourself. You deserve it! Get a massage, energy work, or whatever you are drawn to, and do it on a regular basis. Look at all of the things you do for your body as an investment. There may be a cost in the short term, but they will pay off big in the long run. The better you take care of your body, the more you will physically be able to give to both your business and your clients.

What do you need mentally? You should constantly be growing your mind. I congratulate you on reading this book because that shows you are committed to growing mentally. Keep expanding your knowledge. Keep those neurons firing and sharp. Also make sure you are getting enough rest to stay sharp. Be okay with power naps in the middle of the day. I actually do what I call "reset naps." They are usually about 15 minutes in the mid-afternoon. That is all I need to shake off the lethargy that can creep over me and make me sluggish and tired. I equate it to rebooting a computer--clearing out all the bits of information that build up and slow the system down.

Meditation is another powerful tool for your mental and spiritual well-being. It can refocus your mind and give you greater clarity. Instead of looking at these things as taking time, they are creating greater productivity and creativity, which allows you to accomplish so much more in a much shorter amount of time.

Many of you are "practitioners." Many practitioners do not seek other practitioners. The thought behind that seems to be: "They do the same thing I do, so I will just do it for myself." I am a coach, yet I use several coaches. I use coaches for my body, for my personal life, and for all the aspects of my life, and I use different coaches at different times. I will even use different coaches in the same area to shake things up and get different perspectives. I even use a business coach, which is my "specialty." I know that I CANNOT do for myself what I do for others. I lack the perspective on myself that I bring to others. If I believe in coaching, why would I not have a coach for myself? If you believe in whatever you do, why would you not want someone to do it for or to you? Give yourself the gift of receiving what you do without having to be the one doing it. Be responsible for receiving it and all its benefits.

Finally, remember to do the things you love. Embrace life and whatever that means for you. If you love to read, read. If you love animals, enjoy animals. If you love to hike, hike. If you love to jump out of airplanes, by all means, jump out of airplanes. Do what you love to do so you will love living your life. When you love life, you are much more likely to be around for a long time and able to do what you were meant to do. Take excellent care of yourself in all aspects. Your clients deserve the best possible you, and so do you.

Chapter 16

Spreading Your Light
Where do you go from here?

Now starts the next phase of your journey. If you have created your vision plan, that journey should become much easier. There is a light in the distance that you can move toward that gives you direction and purpose and illuminates the path before you.

Being a Lightpreneur™ is not about the money, but how you deserve to prosper by using your gifts and talents, if not for you, then to honor the giver. *Receive* abundantly so you can continue your work, your journey. *Prosper* so you can expand what you do to levels that you cannot even imagine in this moment. *Remember* that you live in an abundant world and you deserve to receive abundantly for spreading your light.

Accept that the greater the impact you are able to create, if done right, the freer you will be to focus on your passion and your purpose because abundance will follow to free you from the things you do not like to do and that distract you from using your true gifts.

Do what you love, but always remember that part of being a Lightpreneur™ is creating abundance in doing it. Always be aware of how you create that abundance. Constantly look for new ways to add to that abundance and to the impact you create.

Enjoy being a Lightpreneur™ and also the journey itself. I challenge you to wake up each day excited about what you do. Remember that if you are not having fun, fire yourself and start over. It is your business, and you get to create it however you desire.

Being a Lightpreneur™ should bring you joy. It is hard to shine your light in the world with a dark heart. With joy, your light will be able to shine ever brighter. When you decide what your business model should be, make sure it includes the things that bring you joy and allow you to have fun in the journey.

There is a lot of pain and darkness and, because of that, we DO need you now more than ever. Do not allow the seemingly overwhelming troubles of the world to be a burden and put darkness on you. That is counterproductive and the opposite of where you should be coming from. For you to be able to shine the brightest, there must be light and joy on your journey.

Remember to determine your why and use it to drive you forward on your journey. The more powerful your why, the easier it will be to make it past the bumpy parts of the road and the places where FEAR might otherwise dissuade you from your goal. If you find yourself stuck and not moving your business forward, not doing the "right" activities, or lacking focus, go back and ask yourself the question: "Why am I doing this?" That is the key to overcoming anything that can stop you on your journey.

Do not allow the information in this book to overwhelm you. Focus on the twenty percents that will take you where you want to go faster and easier. Take baby steps--what are you going to do first? Second? Next? A journey is a series of steps. Allow yourself to take the journey one step at a time.

Let go of perfection and embrace the evolution--of your business, your journey, and ultimately, the evolution of you. They will and should always be changing and growing. Ready, fire, aim. Constantly try new things. If it works, do more of it. If it doesn't, try something different. When you let go of the need for perfection, you will realize that there already exists perfection in every moment.

Having you read this book is not my goal, but rather that you apply it to make your journey easier and more successful. Use the tools in this book to make your journey easier and even more powerful. After you have implemented the tools presented here into your business, go back and re-read it. There have been many clients who have attended the "Calling All Lightpreneurs™" workshop several times and each time have taken away something they missed or found a new way to apply the same information. Some of the tools may not apply to your business right now, but that may change as your business evolves.

We are looking forward to hearing your success stories of how you are creating impact in the world as a Lightpreneur™. Feel free to share with us how you have used the information in the book to make the world a better, brighter place. Also feel free to let us know about other tools, resources, methods, and anything else that you think other Lightpreneurs™ can use to make their businesses even more impactful. You can contact us through the www.lightpreneurs.com website. Check the website often for new resources to help make your journey easier and your Lightpreneur™ business even brighter.

Yes, Lightpreneur™, you have been called. Called to illuminate the world. Called to help others shine brighter and bolder than ever before. The time is now! Yes, we do need you now more than ever. There is a lot of pain

174

and suffering out there, and people have choices to make. It is time to tip the scale toward love and light and away from fear and darkness. Use your gifts, tools, and talents in ever-expanding ways, creating more and more impact. It is time to leave your mark on this place.

I mentioned how you can lead your customers/clients to water. but you cannot make them drink.

Here is your "water." *Now* it is up to you.

About The Author

Elmas Vincent is committed to serving lightpreneurs™ in being successful in their businesses so they can touch more lives. His key to success with Lightpreneurs™ is keeping things simple. He does not try to impress with big words, but rather, conveys business and success concepts in ways that non-business people can understand and implement. Elmas makes his clients understand that they can do this if they don't allow themselves to become overwhelmed. Then he shows them exactly how to do it. His passion for helping people shines through and lights up the passion in those around him. He is a living testament showing how to come from love and create what you want.

Elmas' education includes an MBA from Tulane University and a BS from Auburn University. He brings a wide variety of experience to the table, having created a range of businesses from retail, to manufacturing, to service. He helped teach one of the first university level courses in entrepreneurship. Being a lightpreneur™ himself, Elmas has a unique style: part crazy professor, part marketing genius, part master coach, and all heart. He has been presenting a wide variety of business talks, seminars, and workshops, as well as doing coaching and consulting for the "practitioner" community for many years.

23018776R00096

Made in the USA
Charleston, SC
07 October 2013